A BOSTON QUARTET

A BOSTON QUARTET

ALAN BALSAM

SPRING IN BACK BAY AND THE PUBLIC GARDEN

SUMMER IN BOSTON COMMON AND DOWNTOWN BOSTON

AUTUMN IN BACK BAY AND THE PUBLIC GARDEN

WINTER IN BOSTON COMMON

In honor of the bicentennial of the independence of the United States of America

Boston Bicentennial Printing
Boston, Massachusetts
Copyright © 2017 Alan Balsam
All rights reserved.

ISBN: 0692913181
ISBN-13: 9780692913185
Library of Congress Control Number: 2017947225
Boston Bicentennial Printing. Delray Beach, Florida

CONTENTS

Preface xiii
Introduction: Boston and the Bicentennial. xv

Spring in Back Bay and the Public Garden 1
    At Longwood a Train Door Would Not Close, Delaying the Trip . . . 3
    On Foot Is the Best Way to See Commonwealth Avenue 4
    Back Bay. 5
    A Walk on Commonwealth Avenue Is a Walk in Boston Proper 7
    A Building with an Entryway with Recessed Arches, and
    Overhead, Cherubs, Gargoyles, and a Window to Nowhere 8
    The Brownstones of Commonwealth Avenue in Back Bay 10
    Back Bay Frontalism. 12
    Preservationism Makes the Automobile an Unwelcome Guest 13
    Another Excess of Preservationism: Unfriendliness to Children. . . . 15
    At the Vendome Complex 16
    Commonwealth Avenue Mall between Berkeley and
    Arlington Streets. 17
    The Public Garden: History and Location 18
    In the Public Garden 19

- Summer in Boston Common 23
  - Origin of Boston Common 24
  - A Scene from an Earlier Time. 24
  - The American Indian Civilization 24
  - Boston Common in the Hands of the Puritans. 26
  - Boston Common as a Public Park. 27
  - On a Clear Day 28
  - Beacon Hill 29
  - Boston Common, a Natural Habitat for Birds 32
  - At the Corner of Tremont and Park Streets. 34
  - Scylla: Historical Site Preservation without Restoration 38
  - Charybdis: Political Stagnation. 41
- Summer in Downtown Boston. 43
  - Downtown Boston. 43
  - Downtown Neighborhoods and Streets 44
  - History and Architecture: Highlights of Downtown Boston. . . . 45
  - Boston Harbor. 47
  - A Walk through History Starts with the Unseen:
    The First Settlement in Massachusetts 47
  - The Second Settlement in New England Was in Boston
    by the Puritans. 48
  - A Walk Back into American History on the Road to
    American Independence. 49
  - Tax Levies and Restrictions of Trade. 52
  - Colonies' Reactions to Tax Levies and Trade Restrictions 52
  - Maintaining a Standing Army and Paying for Quartering
    of British Troops. 53
  - Reactions to Quartering of British Troops. 54
  - The Boston Four: Political Visionary, Shipping Merchant,
    Medical Doctor, and Silversmith 55
    - Samuel Adams, Political Visionary 55
    - John Hancock, Shipping Merchant. 57

  Joseph Warren, Medical Doctor 58
  Paul Revere, Silversmith 59
A Picture of Life in Colonial Times 60
Boston Massacre. 62
Boston Tea Party: British Tea Became Unwelcome in
the American Colonies. 63
The Outbreak of the American Revolution. 64
Battle of Bunker Hill 65
Evacuation Day 66
The Spirit of Resistance to Colonial Rule 67
The American Revolution 68
Destiny Favored Independence for the Colonies. 71
Comments on the Presentation of History 72
In 1876, the Centennial Year of the Independence of the
United States of America 72
A Gift from the Mothers of 1876 to the Daughters of 1976. . . .74
A Visit to Downtown Boston in the Bicentennial Period 75
A Blind Woman Walking in the Streets of Boston. 76
Downtown Crossing. 77
School Street: A City Block That Was an Early
Boston Neighborhood 80
The Rebuilding of Downtown Boston .83
The New and the Old, Side by Side:
The Nexus of Business, Architecture, and History 84
Private Sector Initiatives 85
The Business Landscape: Downtown Skyscrapers. 86
Federal Reserve Bank Building 87
The Financial District. 87
Post Office Square 90
Autumn in Back Bay and the Public Garden 94
 Autumn in New England 94
 Autumn is the Season of the Trees 95

A Trip to Back Bay and the Public Garden in Autumn
Begins on Hammond Street in Newton 98
The Stairs to Building A. 102
The Boston Museum of Fine Arts. 104
Symphony Hall, Boston 106
Back Bay in Modern Times 106
Commercial Development in Back Bay 108
Copley Square Area: A Historical Epicenter of Back Bay 108
Boston Public Library. 110
The Origin of Copley Square 111
The Museum of Fine Arts: A Central Element in
Copley Square Departs. 113
Copley Square Today 114
Skyscrapers in Back Bay 114
The John Hancock Tower: One of Three John Hancock
Buildings in Boston 115
The Advantages and Disadvantages of a Northeast Exposure 115
A Battle between Nature and a Skyscraper:
The Winds versus the Windows 116
Park Square 117
Park Square in the Twentieth Century: from Rags to Riches 118
Park Square at the Time of the Bicentennial 120
Autumn in Boston 121
A Walk in the Public Garden in Autumn 122
Public Garden Trees in Autumn 123
Winter in Boston Common 128
A Walk through Boston Common on a Very Cold Day 129
The Martyrs of the Ecclesiastical Laws of the Puritans 130
Bigotry in Public Forums 131
Preservation of Historical Places Emphasizing Functionality 133

Pride in Historical Preservation. 134
Boston Common and the First Snow of Winter 134
Beacon Hill in Winter 136
Storms and Stresses of Winter. 137
The Blizzard of 1978 138
A Warming Trend in Winter Is a Prelude to Spring. 140
Centennial Anniversaries of United States Independence 142

References 149
Back Bay History and Architecture. 149
Commonwealth Avenue 150
Boston Vendome Hotel and Its Lighting Consultant,
Thomas A. Edison 151
Boylston Street 152
Copley Square and Vicinity 153
Old South Church 153
The Three John Hancock Buildings 153
Boston Public Garden. 155
Boston Common 157
Park Square 159
Beacon Hill 160
History of Boston and Massachusetts Bay Colony 161
    Precolonial Times: Indians of the Algonquian Nation. 161
    Early Colonial Times (1620–1760): Pilgrims 161
    William Blaxton, First English Settler on the Shawmut
    Peninsula 163
    Puritans 163
    Life in Colonial America. 165
    Boston from 1765 to 1775: A Cauldron of Discontent
    in the Prelude to the American Revolution 167

Boston Patriots...167
    Samuel Adams, Politician........................167
    John Hancock, Merchant.........................169
    Joseph Warren, Physician.......................171
    Paul Revere, Silversmith........................171
British Colonial Administrators.......................173
    Francis Bernard, Governor of Massachusetts Bay Colony....173
    Thomas Gage, General and Governor of
    Massachusetts Bay Colony.......................175
British Military Officers.............................175
    John Burgoyne, General.........................175
    Henry Clinton, General.........................176
    Samuel Graves, Admiral.........................177
    William Howe, General..........................177
British Monarch.......................................180
    George III, King of England....................180
Conflicts in Massachusetts Bay Colony before the Revolution...183
    Boston Massacre................................183
    Boston Tea Party...............................185
    Battles of Lexington and Concord...............187
    Battle of Bunker Hill..........................190
    American Revolution............................191
Honored Guests in Boston—George Washington,
Benjamin Franklin, and Alexander Hamilton: Founding
Fathers from Virginia, Pennsylvania, and New York..........192
    George Washington: Commander-in-Chief,
    Continental Army, and First President of the United States...192
    Benjamin Franklin: Publisher, Scientist, and Diplomat....197
    Alexander Hamilton, Father of United States Federalist
    Economic System................................202

Downtown Boston and the Harbor 208
　　　　School Street. 208
　　　　Downtown Crossing. 209
　　Alexander Graham Bell. 211
　　The Financial District. 213
　　Post Office Square, Art Deco Design and Architecture 214
　　Boston Harbor 216
　　Old City Hall and New City Hall 217
　　Old and New Massachusetts State Houses 218
About the Author. 221
Index 223

PREFACE

In this writing, I have assembled some remembrances of the city of Boston from the decade starting with the bicentennial of the independence of our country, celebrated on July 4, 1976. The impressions I describe derive from multiple encounters with places over a considerable period of time to approximately 1997. For the purpose of presentation, however, the impressions are presented in a narrative of visits along a few selected routes through Boston. The focal points of interest are two neighborhoods in the city, Back Bay and Downtown, and the two parks, the Public Garden and the Boston Common, that lie between them.

The essay is divided into four parts, each describing one or more of these locations in a particular season of the year. Depictions of places and people of the area are based on a mixture of personal observations, experiences and reflections, and historical vignettes. In most instances, the historical background presented derives from the writings of the times discussed. In a few, however, in the absence of historical information, I have taken literary license and instead used metaphor and allegory to capture the spirit of an era.

Any city's character is a complex weaving of distinguishing features. Like threads in a tapestry, those features are often so tightly intertwined that separating one from the others for close inspection can be difficult. In considering Boston, a city that has developed over several hundred years, I examine subjects that seem worlds apart: nature, the seasons, architecture, urban development, and American history, focusing on colonial times up to the outbreak of the American Revolution. However, each is an important element in Boston's urban tapestry.

A portrait of a place in words reveals not only the subject's physical attributes but often its underlying spiritual character. Mood colorings are evoked as well, such as those related to seasonal changes or historical events. Views presented here about the significance and implications of historical events are mostly those of the author, who in the spirit of fairness, has made every effort to create a balanced picture, considering the points of view of all parties involved. Additional information about historical characters and events may be found in the references listed at the end of the essay.

A treatise that includes a discussion of urban development should always evaluate the social and political factors that played a role as well as government policy. The government has the responsibility to promote and oversee development in residential, commercial, and public real estate, including parks. Attitudes and policies that hinder progress should be identified and challenged. Any critique rendered here, mostly calling for a more vigorous and dynamic approach, is with constructive intent. For example, in the instance of conservation of history, preservation of historically important sites is certainly a worthy goal, but it must never be a central goal. The past is only a peripheral issue, and the relics of the past may be interesting, but the challenges of the present and the future are much more important.

INTRODUCTION: BOSTON AND THE BICENTENNIAL

We celebrate our independence every year on July 4, the anniversary of the day in 1776 when all thirteen colonies agreed that colonial rule must end, by any means necessary, including military force. It was a big step forward in our history, and there was an unusual display of unity among the colonies, which were unrelated, with diverse economies and different political interests. The factors that prompted the colonies to take that step are summarized in the Declaration of Independence, which was approved, signed, and promulgated that day by the Second Continental Congress. July 4, 1776, was not the actual date of our independence—that came later, after the final battle of the war on October 19, 1781, when the British surrendered at Yorktown in the colony of Virginia. But in a way, it is very reasonable that we link our independence to that day in history, as firm resolve is always needed to make great things happen. That certainly was a day of firm resolve and was a momentous decision for our nation.

At the time of the Second Continental Congress, there was an active rebellion in Boston and Massachusetts Bay Colony. This made the town and the colony the birthplace of the American Revolution. Boston, a port city and a center of trade between Europe and the colonies, had been under British military occupation since 1768. Intense dissatisfaction with tariffs and trade restrictions, other abuses of colonial rule, and the heavy hand of the occupation sparked the armed resistance.

In celebrating our independence, it is the American Revolution itself that has to be emphasized. Of course, we cherish the day in our nation's history on which the colonies reached common ground in declaring their independence from Britain. But making resolutions stating that circumstances were intolerable was only an acknowledgment of what was already widely perceived at the time. Conflicts with Britain arising in the context of abuses of its colonial power had been experienced throughout the colonies but most keenly in Boston, which was under occupation by British troops. A rebellion had been evolving a few years earlier in Massachusetts Bay Colony, and it reached a climax in 1775 with the first battles of the as-yet undeclared war.

In celebrating our independence, we must give credit where it is due. We owe a debt of gratitude to the people who realized very early that obeisance to a foreign colonial power offered no future for our country. And there was a growing consensus that words alone would not bring about the departure of the oppressors—only actions. No words, moral reasoning, or passive resistance could move the colonial power one inch, as the British Empire was a colossus that would not be moved. It was the call to arms and the revolution that succeeded in removing it. We celebrate the acts that led to the armed struggle and the victories that led to the defeat of the colonial power. Acts such as throwing British tea into Boston Harbor, stockpiling of arms in Concord, the call to arms, and the first musket shot fired by the patriots in combat in Concord—the "shot heard round the world," as Emerson called it—that must be celebrated. The battles of Lexington, Concord, and Bunker Hill also have to be celebrated. They led to the declaration of war that is implicit in the Declaration of Independence.

There is only one war in our history where our victory can be considered by every American as having brought personal emancipation and fundamental change in our prospects as a people—the American Revolution. At the time, however, no citizen of this country could possibly have realized the enormous effect the revolution would have on the opportunities for future generations. That war brought about the gift of independence.

There is a tradition of celebrating anniversaries by one-hundred-year periods or centennials. You could celebrate a centennial in different ways. On the one hand, you could relate the story of the events that led to the uprising and those connected to the revolution itself as there is much to be learned from those events. In addition, you could review what has been accomplished in our country in the one hundred years since the last centennial. Another approach is to examine the environment at the time of the centennial anniversary, in this instance the bicentennial, in search of hints of the past. Such hints often do not present in an orderly manner, so it is important to bring order to disparate elements so that the picture may emerge.

SPRING IN BACK BAY AND THE PUBLIC GARDEN

Daffodils, the yellow sentinels of spring, had come and gone in Back Bay; dogwoods and magnolias, white and pink, had peaked on Commonwealth Avenue; and spring had appeared in earnest in Boston's Public Garden. That day my destination was Back Bay and the Public Garden. The trip to Back Bay and the Public Garden began at the T Station in Chestnut Hill.

As I drove across the bridge on Hammond Street and turned right, driving down the hill into the Chestnut Hill T station parking lot, I completed an outline of the itinerary for my trip in my mind. It was a beautiful and clear spring day, and my plan was to take the T to Kenmore and walk the rest of the way along Commonwealth Avenue to the Public Garden. The visit would bring me through certain parts of the Emerald Necklace, a group of parks, ponds, and riverbank greenways that wind like a necklace through Boston and Brookline. The group starts with Boston Common and the Public Garden, continues along Back Bay in Commonwealth Mall, turns at the Fens, and continues along the Riverway in Boston. It crosses the border into Brookline through Olmstead Park, continues through Jamaica Plain to Jamaica

Pond, and follows the Jamaicaway to the Arborway, Arnold Arboretum, and finally Franklin Park. On that day my plan was to visit three links in the Emerald Necklace: the Riverway, Commonwealth Avenue Mall, and the Public Garden. The train would take me through the Riverway, and I would then walk along Commonwealth Avenue next to the mall and then to the Public Garden.

It was a Sunday, and the T station parking lot was mostly empty, just a few cars here and there of people who started their trip earlier. In contrast, during the week, the parking lot generally was full, and there was the hustle and bustle of people heading inbound to work destinations, including Back Bay and Downtown. On that day, however, all was quiet, and there was nobody waiting for the trains on the outbound side, which is completely open, or the inbound side, with the waiting area in a roofed enclosure. The site was below street level, and it was a weekend day. The signs of spring had come to Chestnut Hill, and the leafy canopies of the trees near the station were full. There was little sound of traffic, but the music of spring was in the air that morning with the chirping of songbirds. The lyrical notes of a chorus of buntings, warblers, and wrens nearby, however, were brusquely interrupted by staccato sounds—the tap-tap-tap of a lone pileated woodpecker not too far in the distance.

I thought that I might have to wait longer than usual for the train, and I was prepared to do that, but as soon as I crossed the tracks to the inbound side, the birds became quiet, and the piercing screech of wheels of an approaching train turning in the distance broke the silence. I liked the Riverside branch of the Green Line, and I had taken the trip inbound through Newton and Brookline many times before. There was always some new discovery to be made from the interior of the train. The train would emerge from below street level, providing excellent views of the verdant surroundings.

The train took me through the lowlands around Chestnut Hill Reservoir, which could not be seen, but it continued to higher elevations in Brookline starting at the nearby Reservoir T station. Having emerged from one parking lot at the Chestnut Hill T station, I entered another at the Reservoir station, which was at the confluence of an additional branch and had a parking lot of its own, not for automobiles but for trains. Then, heading east, there were expansive northerly views of Brookline and beyond, including many children's playgrounds. The T cars had wide windows; I could see the outdoors best standing, and I was very experienced at standing. Slow train speeds made the views even more distinct. The path of the train took a sharp turn to the north at Brookline Village, winding its way along the Riverway, past Longwood and Fenway, and on into Kenmore.

AT LONGWOOD A TRAIN DOOR WOULD NOT CLOSE, DELAYING THE TRIP

That day, the ride went very smoothly until the train reached Longwood. There, someone got on the train in the car I was in, but the door would not close. I had a feeling that the driver would know how to fix it. I was sitting opposite the door, and when it opened, I could make out the LONGWOOD station sign. During the delay, I caught a glimpse of some interesting Riverway maples through the doorway, and my thoughts turned to trees.

Not too far away from the station to the east is Beech Road in Brookline, which has a small park filled with beech trees, a park like no other I have ever seen. The park is in a rectangular median, with houses on either side of the street. A walk along Beech Road is a visit to a world of immense beauty and power. Even just the thought of it has a profound effect. The best time to appreciate the essence of those trees is in late winter or very early spring when they are leafless. The grand beeches planted in the central quadrangle are statuesque and remind me of a herd of elephants frozen in space. The gray of the smooth bark of the trees commands attention, and their tortuous limbs and roots seem to reach out. The breadth of the trunks is absolutely astounding. In summer the trees are completely enveloped in a leafy canopy that extends like a woman's gown flowing to the ground.

While my thoughts were on Beech Road, the motorman came and gave the door a push, and it closed immediately thereafter. The train resumed moving shortly after that.

ON FOOT IS THE BEST WAY TO SEE COMMONWEALTH AVENUE

Sometimes what people do is more related to inclination than to any pragmatic purpose. I enjoy walking, for short or long distances, and I prefer walking to other means of transportation. I was accustomed to what I called using my legs for transportation. So the decision to exit the T at Kenmore was a good choice—walking was the better option because there is no comparison to the experience it provides, and walking uncovers an almost infinite number of interesting sights than would a ride on the local T under the streets of Back Bay. Some people say you can get from Kenmore Square to Arlington Street faster by walking than by the T. Let's just say that the trip time is comparable if you are a strong walker and in a hurry. But that day I was in no hurry; hence, I decided to make my way to the park on foot. I walked past Charlesgate East down Commonwealth Avenue on the southern, or Newbury Street, side, heading toward Downtown. That is the inbound direction of the street. For some reason, whenever I walked in that direction, I always walked on that side of the avenue.

BACK BAY

Back Bay is a Boston neighborhood that is bordered on the west by Charlesgate East, on the east by Arlington Street, on the north by the Charles River, and on the south by the Massachusetts Turnpike. Its outline has the shape of a trapezoid tipped over on its long arm and positioned in an east to west direction, with the base being Arlington Street, the top Charlesgate East, the short straight arm the Charles riverbank and the long arm the turnpike. There is a large rectangle composed of Commonwealth Avenue at its center. Flanking it on the north side are Marlborough Street and Beacon Street, and on the south side, Newbury Street and Boylston Street. The traffic flow on Commonwealth is bidirectional, and on the neighboring streets to the north and the south it is unidirectional.

The land on which Back Bay is built was the site of tidal flats of the Charles River, which had to be filled before anything could be built on it. At high tide, the flats were completely flooded, and the area was a shallow bay; and at low tide, the marshes were exposed. Land reclamation began with planning in the early part of the nineteenth century and continued with construction during the second half of the century. The process of filling in marshes was not new. As a given area is built up, thought is given to the possibility of developing land for building use and filling very shallow water areas is a logical choice. In about 1814 there was a large project called Mildam that was designed to provide power for mills by separating the Charles from the Back Bay marshes along with a more direct road from Boston to Watertown. That project was not a financial success, and a new plan to fill in Back Bay was developed. Around 1830, Mill Pond was filled, adding an area of about fifty acres of buildable land to Boston.

In 1857, the filling of Back Bay commenced, and 450 acres were reclaimed with fill brought from Needham, Massachusetts. On terra firma, railroad tracks were extended about nine miles to the quarries of Needham, and gravel and other types of fill arrived in thirty-five-car trains to Back Bay every three-quarters of an hour. Streets were filled on average to grade 17, which denotes that number of feet above low tide level. Lots were filled at least to grade 12, a level required for basements to be constructed. A setback of twenty feet from building to street was considered generous at the time.

Three years later the filling of the area reached Clarendon Street and by 1870, Exeter Street. In 1882, the filling of Back Bay was complete, having reached Charlesgate East. During that period of about twenty-five years, buildings were constructed on filled sites in Back Bay. An early photograph of the area called *Commonwealth Avenue in Process, 1872*, shows the beginnings of the mall and only a handful of attached buildings interspersed along the Marlborough Street side of the avenue. Very little construction is shown on the avenue itself and much more along the intersecting streets and on Marlborough Street and Beacon Street.

The Charles River is clearly seen behind the construction, with no bridges connecting Boston to Cambridge. Most bridges across the Charles were constructed starting the last decade of the nineteenth century; the Harvard Bridge, the first and longest bridge across the Charles, connecting Back Bay and Cambridge, was completed in 1890. The Esplanade was created along the bank of the Charles River and Storrow Drive was later added to facilitate east-west vehicular traffic.

The area of Back Bay that is explored here is Commonwealth Avenue, with Marlborough and Beacon Streets on the north and Newbury and Boylston Streets on the south. All five streets are parallel, running east to west, and are intersected by streets that run north to south. The pattern is a grid, which is typical of man-made streets. In contrast, the streets in downtown Boston are circular, as they evolved according to an older pattern.

A WALK ON COMMONWEALTH AVENUE IS A WALK IN BOSTON PROPER

At the time of the revolution, many mercantilists specializing in the shipping trade lived in Cambridge and Boston and considered themselves British subjects loyal to Britain. They were called Tories, or loyalists, and their loyalty was based more on custom and deference to authority rather than political persuasion, which held true even to a greater extent for the uncommitted or those who sympathized with the loyalists. By most, the act of rebellion was considered anathema, but nonetheless the causes that favored that option were considered to be worthy. Although from the historical perspective of our country they were on the wrong side in the conflict, they had great talents in business, and they were the main builders of commerce in the area, mostly import and export. From an architectural perspective in particular, they were builders par excellence, and we can see that in the examples of architecture that survive from that period. Over a century later, their successors moved to Boston, and they continued to develop business and industry in the area. Brahmins—later-generation Tories—were Bostonians who specialized in mercantilism. They were known for their business and educational accomplishments and for their prejudices as well. However, one shouldn't permit Brahmin prejudices to detract from their accomplishments. There is much to admire in their legacy of achievements. "Boston Proper" was the term given to their way of doing things, which was meticulous and with a heavy English influence.

With the ascendancy of the Brahmins and the English influence, historical reference to the Boston patriots was minimized. None of the Boston patriots were admitted to Back Bay or the Public Garden, either in street names or statuary. It was as if the neighborhood were a reunion with the British Empire. It became permissible to admit just about anybody with some political currency except the patriots. It is an irony of history that the only solid ground in the area was that on which the patriots stood—Back Bay consisted of uninhabitable marshes. High conservancy in Back Bay has kept that pattern going to this very day. However, from a historical standpoint you could argue that preserving downtown Boston was far more important than preserving Back Bay. Downtown is the spirit of our independence, while Back Bay is a visitation by the English.

Commonwealth Avenue is divided by a large parklike median called Commonwealth Mall, with a central path that has benches and statuary flanked by trees in a grassy area on either side. The design emulated that used in the rebuilding of Paris, featuring expansive tree-lined avenues, central parks, and geometric street patterns. There is certain quietude to the park as there is limited space in the adjacent street lanes for traffic, which is also slowed by traffic lights, and the trees serve to buffer the din. The trees in the mall are substantial, tall, and impressive leafy deciduous specimens. In contrast, the street trees, which are located alongside the brownstones, are mostly bush trees that are kept at a low height.

The outbound avenue lane is on the Marlborough Street side of the Avenue, which overall is a more desirable location, and its northern exposure provides ample shade for the dogwoods and the magnolias to bloom in the spring. As a general rule, the streets that are closest to the picturesque Charles River and most remote from the commercial streets, Newbury and Boylston, are the most desirable residential location.

A BUILDING WITH AN ENTRYWAY WITH RECESSED ARCHES, AND OVERHEAD, CHERUBS, GARGOYLES, AND A WINDOW TO NOWHERE

I first walked past a very ornate mansion at the corner of Hereford Street. That building is so unusual that it seems like a creation from a different world. I knew that building very well because the Boston Evening Clinic was located there, and I had served as a general doctor taking sick call there when I first came to Boston. The mansion was built of white stone in the Romanesque Revival style that was popular starting around 1870. It appears to have a very continental European architectural influence, so I could understand that there would be few examples of that since Back Bay has such a heavy English influence. Many object to its ornamentation, regarding it as excessive. I disagree with that notion; although it has a heavy ornateness, the features are balanced and generally pleasing to the eye. The facade had a deeply recessed arched entryway in the central element. Above that, at the second story, is a flat filigree veranda partition at the base of two long vertical windows and at the third story a circular projecting veranda at the base of two shorter windows. Above that is a gable in the mansard roof with a pair of windows flanked by cherubs and topped by a rectangular stone frame that has a window to nowhere and finials above that. The appellation "window to nowhere" is one I give to a window that is present in a decorative piece—an attempt to create decorative symmetry—but does not function as a window. It also shows that there are lapses in following the ancient and intuitive architectural principle "Form follows function" in architectural development.

Although the external ornateness is not necessarily related to the purpose of the building, my feeling is that for the building's use as a clinic in modern times there was limited functionality. That was related to the residential character and the age of the building. In this and in many other ornate buildings there are pieces that were added only for artistic balance. To either side of the central element are visually dominant, large projecting bay windows with a single gable of similar design above that. Throughout the facade, cherubs and gargoyle heads decorate the exterior wall.

In Back Bay it is rare to see more than one side of a building, and corner buildings only show the front and one side. The Hereford Street side of the building has very different structural and ornamental details. Here the decorative elements unfold beginning on the second story, which weakens the architectural design as the undecorated stone base has only a mundane visual impact. The general style on the side facade of the building features elements in the same style. In the central motif, starting at the second story, is a large and ornate concrete triple bay window extension and at its base is a shallow veranda with a multisegmented partition that features shield patterns. Perched atop the partition on either side are animal statues. A large stone wreath serves as a capital for the bay window. Above that is a rectangular stone gable enclosing two windows and above that is a rectangular element with a window to nowhere with finials above and to the side. Flanking the central element are two cylindrical towers with conical roofs. The lateral elements include additional bay windows, one on either side.

THE BROWNSTONES OF COMMONWEALTH AVENUE IN BACK BAY

Then I walked past a seemingly endless array of ornate residential structures made of stone. You could call them brownstone, whitestone, graystone, or orangestone buildings, each with very different details but many sharing the same style. The architectural pattern of the buildings bears a heavy English influence from the Victorian era. The style emphasizes sharp corners and simplicity overall. I prefer the more ornate styles of the French and the Italian architectural genres of the period. The buildings on the Newbury side of the Avenue are overall of lesser quality than on the Marlborough side, and this follows a general pattern of higher residential quality buildings on the streets that are closer to the Charles River. The buildings are attached one to another, and it is difficult to focus on the details of any single one while walking. I found that on my right side their images seemed to merge into a large multishaded wall of geometric shapes reminiscent of a Cezanne landscape portrait. The presentation of multiple forms, colors, and styles in a very congested space brought to mind a strange metaphor—it was as if the paintings in the galleries on Newbury Street were taken off the show walls, unframed and placed one next to another, creating a mélange of colors and shapes. Also, while walking, I would catch glimpses of unaesthetic externalities: blotches of ivy covering some buildings, corroded copper fixtures, discordant roof additions, poorly matched sizing, misplaced wide concrete stairs to brownstones, and traffic signs connected to streetlamps, all of which are indecorous visual disturbances in an otherwise beautiful scene. I could never understand why there are so many examples of poorly designed stairwells attached to the brownstones. In many instances they seem to have been added as an afterthought. The worst among those have a very steep rise, no landings, and no railings.

If I owned a brownstone in Back Bay, I would consider it a good investment to have a proper stairwell with functional and aesthetically pleasing features. Standing in the way of correcting architectural flaws is a significant problem associated with unreasonable conservation of the environment: it preserves the bad with the good. That approach gives no consideration to the possibility that the original design may have been poor and could benefit from improvement. Architecture is an evolving art and science, and when it is not permitted to change, it stagnates. The guidelines of the Back Bay Architectural Commission refer to entryways, porticos, porches, and stoops with the admonition that they should not be "altered, removed, or enclosed." Ill repair of the stairs, however, is another issue, and the weather is a factor, leading to crumbling of the stairs, requiring reconstruction. Also, most of the rooftop additions seem to detract from the buildings' general appearance as they disturb the continuity of design. The majority of those are on the south side of the avenue, which overall seems more eclectic and architecturally weaker than the north side.

At the time Back Bay was constructed, brownstone was a common type of stone used for building attached multifamily dwellings. Its use for that purpose was prevalent in New York, Philadelphia, and many other cities along the East Coast, starting about the mid-1800s. The stone used in the building construction, sandstone, was cheaper than other, more sturdy forms, such as granite and marble, and over time the technique for producing the stone improved and a higher quality product was produced. The sandstone is brown and derives from quarries along the Connecticut River. The most common variety is Portland brownstone, which comes from a quarry in Portland, Connecticut. It is important to note that the stone being less sturdy is subject to the effects of wear, and therefore construction maintenance and repair is important. I learned this when a kind gentleman mentioned to me that in the office building I owned, which had a brownstone exterior, there was a crack in the cornice at the corner. I thanked him and immediately had it repaired.

BACK BAY FRONTALISM

On considering the brownstones, I realized that in most instances you only see the front of each building and nothing of the sides or back. A model for that is early Egyptian art, which features a view of the front but none of any other side. This is an early artistic style called frontalism. Many fine examples of this style can be enjoyed in the Egyptian wing of the Museum of Fine Arts, Boston. From an architectural point of view, I consider brownstone frontalism a significant limitation. It seems that all of the effort on the exterior of the building is concentrated on the front of the building, and that obviously is an economic compromise and benefit to the builders as they are relieved of any expenditure in decorating the sides or the back of the building. It also has a detrimental effect to the interior of the building as it tends to have less natural light with windows only in the front and back. Also, with attached structures, there is very little room for trees. They have to be small and once again, when they are in front of the structure, you have only a unidimensional view of them.

Walking down the avenue, I occasionally felt a sense of monotony in the wall of brownstones. Commonwealth Mall, with its statuary in the tree-lined median, provided welcome relief from that feeling. Unfortunately, when the foliage is full, many of the statues on their pedestals are obscured by leafy canopies. Good views of those, however, are obtained from the upper stories of the brownstones. At the corners, the statues are open to view and easily seen from multiple vantage points.

PRESERVATIONISM MAKES THE AUTOMOBILE AN UNWELCOME GUEST

By the very early 1900s, the building of Back Bay was completed. The area has been designated a national historical landmark as it provides many fine examples of Victorian and Continental architecture of the 1800s. "Preservationism" is a term that I use to describe attempts to preserve the historical character of the man-made environment. In the instance of Back Bay, preservationism refers mostly to the architectural aspects of the neighborhood. In many ways, the residential neighborhood has been frozen in time because of the tendency to preserve buildings from the past by imposing restrictions on any architectural changes. Many would say that this is a worthwhile endeavor. Others would counter that it is subject to excesses, and furthermore, places too many constraints on the people who live in the area that is subject to the restrictions. With respect to buildings and historical sites, it involves very strict zoning, and any change in buildings requires architectural review and approval. Such review and approval, however, is no guarantee that the result will be aesthetically pleasing as there is often a difference between what a structure looks like on paper and what it looks like when it is built. We can find many examples of changes that have been approved that appear awkward and out of place in relation to neighboring structures. From a philosophical standpoint, one can say that excess preservationism interferes with normal architectural evolution that otherwise would occur and perhaps better serve the needs of society and its members.

Automobiles with gasoline-powered engines were starting to be produced in the second half of the first decade of the twentieth century. Model T Fords, the first mass-produced automobiles, started rolling out of the factories in 1907 and rapidly gained popularity. The automobile is clearly one of the most brilliant inventions known to mankind. The automobile as a means of personal transportation is an instrument of individual freedom bringing one to faraway places and to a world of new experiences.

One of the responsibilities of ownership of an automobile has always been finding a place to park it. However, Back Bay is inhospitable to parking an automobile. The brownstones are attached, as are most of the other buildings, and in mostly residential areas there are no garages. The back alleys are narrow with room only for a few parking spaces. In addition, as time moved on, the situation has grown worse because there are more cars and little increase in the number of parking spaces. As a consequence of the imbalance of supply and demand, parking spaces are sold for large sums of money and prices have been escalating continuously. In 2009, two Back Bay alley parking spaces sold for the sum of $560,000, a record amount. The scarcity of parking tends to be worsened by a strong legacy of preservationism, so that it is difficult to create something new like a parking garage in a historically preserved location. And preservationism makes the cost of owning an automobile rise because of the expense of parking.

Many residents of Back Bay do not own an automobile, a deficiency condition that may be called "carless in Back Bay." When Saturday and Sunday come around, you can sit at a table in an outdoor café or walk past historical and architectural delights, but for residents there is a need to move beyond the confines of the everyday experience of the neighborhood, to explore new places and seek out the natural environment that ready access to a car can satisfy. And there is no question whatsoever that being carless in Back Bay has unfavorable consequences for the person, most important being parochialism.

Dr. Murray Gavel, my dentist on Marlborough Street, told me he had a patient in the neighborhood who ordered a custom-made Rolls-Royce with some special features that had been explained to him when the sale was arranged. Apparently, it would have picnic paraphernalia, including a serving tray and an ice-cooled bucket, in a compartment in the back passenger area that could be removed for use and then folded and put back into place. However, when the car was delivered from the factory, lo and behold, no picnic apparatus. The buyer, unfazed by the setback, requested that it be sent back, and in about a month the properly equipped car was delivered. On hearing that story, I thought, *All that is well and good, but where would you want to park a Rolls-Royce in Back Bay?* Not in the back alleys and not in a parking garage and certainly not on the street. That would be the last place you would want it to be. On that day, while walking down Commonwealth Avenue, that story came to mind and confirmed my theory: as far as I could see, there were no Rolls-Royce automobiles parked on the street.

ANOTHER EXCESS OF PRESERVATIONISM: UNFRIENDLINESS TO CHILDREN

Another downside of preservationism is unfriendliness to children. One can't escape that conclusion in walking down Commonwealth Avenue. Any environment that does not support the automobile is unfriendly to children. Moreover, there are no niche children's parks and little that would attract their interest in Commonwealth Mall. The galleries and shops of Newbury Street and the stores on Boylston Street provide little of interest to a child. At the time that the residential area of Back Bay was conceived and constructed it appears that little attention was paid to the needs of children in the environment. This is a problem that must be remedied.

AT THE VENDOME COMPLEX

Walking past the rebuilt Vendome Complex, I headed toward the Arlington Street entrance to the park. The Boston Vendome Hotel, its predecessor, was built in 1871, modeled after a hotel in Paris by the same name. The hotel occupied a location at the corner of Commonwealth Avenue and Dartmouth Street, and it was built in the French Second Empire style. The Vendome of 1871 is a very fine example of the charm and beauty of the French architectural style. In its location it provided a welcome relief from the English Victorian style, which favored a simpler and slightly austere presentation. Also, its white stone exterior presented a needed interruption from the monotony of the brownstones. It is curious that the hotel was built on a residential street. However, at the time hotels were often used as residences. The placement of the Vendome in a residential location was consistent with its use at the time. In keeping with that notion, over one hundred years later, a largely residential complex occupies the site.

At the time it was built, Back Bay was largely empty, as can be seen in the photo of the area titled *Back Bay in Process*. About a decade later, a large change was to occur in the building. In 1881, the world was in the midst of a milestone change—it was the advent of the era of electricity. The hotel was expanded that year, and electricity was added, making it the first hotel in the city to have electric lighting. During the previous decade, electricity had come into use for street lighting and very high voltage arc lamps were used. However, interior lighting with those lamps was not possible because the high voltage was a danger. The hotel hired a consultant, Thomas Alva Edison, who had invented the incandescent light bulb for indoor lighting two years earlier, to evaluate the building's interior lighting.

In the 1881 reconstruction of the hotel, a large extension was added to the west of the original structure. The off-center element with the pyramidal roof was the first part of the extension, and it had a recessed entryway. Sadly, on July 17, 1972, during an attempt to preserve and renovate the historical structure in its 101st year, it fell victim to a tragic fire that destroyed the entire building and claimed the lives of nine firefighters. Built in its place was the Vendome Complex, an architecturally pleasing structure that houses condominium apartments and a restaurant. Its general features are very reminiscent of the hotel, including a dominant off-center element with a pyramidal roof facing the avenue, similar to that appearing in the western extension to the hotel built in 1881, and with the same number of stories. I would say that in Back Bay, I find no site more interesting and attractive than the Vendome. The corner location and the breadth of Dartmouth Street make that site most impressive. The setback from the avenue is generously proportioned, and the building has limited height, presenting an interesting long horizontal presence. On July 4, you can watch the fireworks display in a more intimate and less congested setting than the riverbank of the Charles. The width of Dartmouth Street and its location provides great views of the display. I could linger at that site many hours, admiring its great beauty from various perspectives.

COMMONWEALTH AVENUE MALL BETWEEN BERKELEY AND ARLINGTON STREETS

I made my way down the avenue, and at the corner of Berkeley Street I entered the mall, heading to Arlington Street to view the statue of

Alexander Hamilton, which was the first statue placed in Commonwealth Mall in 1865. The work, sculpted in granite by William Rimmer, a physician, stands close to the entrance to the Public Garden and faces the statue of George Washington. The statue of Hamilton in formal attire of the day is on a high pedestal reaching an impressive height, and is shaded by a canopy of treetops on both sides. The statue has a frontal emphasis, facing directly forward. Hamilton, the first secretary of the Treasury, was the grand architect of federalism, the foundation of the economic prosperity of our country. Placing a statue of Hamilton at the head of Back Bay seems appropriate as it is symbolic of the neighborhood's prosperity. Hamilton's picture is featured on the ten-dollar bill. That honor is based upon the importance of his contributions to the monetary system, which would also justify having his picture on all paper currency denominations. The pictures of former presidents on various dollar bill denominations honor important contributions they made to the country, unrelated to the monetary system.

THE PUBLIC GARDEN: HISTORY AND LOCATION

The Public Garden was built in 1862 during the time of active reclamation of Back Bay. It was conceived as a botanical garden in 1837 by a local philanthropist, Horace Gray, but the project got ensnared in the Boston legislative process—political wrangling—and was delayed almost thirty years until Back Bay was being actively built. Notwithstanding the delay, in keeping with the history of politics, the sign at the entrance to the park proclaims: PUBLIC GARDEN, 1837. An 1837 drawing of Park Square and surroundings shows that, at the time, the Charles River estuary covered the area of today's Public Garden. Historical accuracy aside, the garden is a great source of pride for the city of Boston, and we all know that pride often gives rise to hyperbole.

The Public Garden was designed by landscape architect George F. Meacham. The site is rectangular and comprises twenty-four acres just west of Boston Common. The park is bordered on its longer sides on the west by Arlington Street and on the east by Charles Street. On its shorter sides it is bordered by Beacon Street on the north and Boylston Street on the south. The park has two main entryways, one on Arlington Street and the other on Charles Street. The Public Garden seems very properly located at that site, serving as an extension of Back Bay and a gateway to the Boston Common and Beacon Hill. You could say that Back Bay and the Public Garden fit like a hand in a glove. Moreover, the ornamental design and the artistic flair of the former continue in the latter.

Just beyond the Arlington Street entryway entrance to the Public Garden is a statue by Thomas Ball of George Washington riding on a horse. Washington is dressed in military uniform, and the statue honors his role as commander in chief of the Continental army. In March 1776, Washington brought artillery to Dorchester Heights south of the city, and the British decided to evacuate Boston and sail to the naval fleet's home base in Halifax, Nova Scotia.

IN THE PUBLIC GARDEN

The late morning April air had a New England chill to it, and standing at the threshold of the Public Garden, I was about to enter a world of man-made order and tranquil beauty. The din of traffic subsided immediately as I walked through the gateway to the park, as there is a descent to below street level. The park is rectangular; there are only a few pathways to traverse, and the man-made lake is at its center. The perimeter is marked by a decorative low-set wrought-iron partition, which has no equal in any park in the country. The ornamental fence is composed of iron pickets with simple finials, alternating in height and shape, attached to thick iron picket-like posts, each of which stands on a granite pedestal and displays an intricate lotus leaf finial. The thick posts appear at intervals of one after every seventeen narrow pickets. The entrances to the Public Garden have granite rectangular columns, each with a concrete ball mounted at the top. The profusion of color in the annual and perennial ground flowers, the well-manicured lawns, common and exotic trees, and the low walking suspension bridge across the lake add to its attraction to visitors.

The main detraction is the feeling that the placement of the elements is not the work of nature but that of man, as they unfold in a highly structured, orderly manner. Other detractions include a profusion of uninteresting statuary and puerile elements that appear to reflect political tinkering.

I walked past the grand equestrian statue of Washington and took a sharp right turn to a path heading toward the Boylston Street border, where the stately elms tower over a wide walking path. I've always been partial to that portion of the Public Garden that brings the park and the Boylston Street side by side, separated only by a low wrought-iron partition. I could stand in the park and enjoy the sights and noises of the outside street and the bucolic quietude within at the same time. With full foliage atop the elms, scarcely a ray of sunlight pierces through, and the walking path is completely shaded. I then retraced my steps, headed back to the entrance, and walked on a gradual incline to the flat portion of the suspension bridge. I was only one of many people walking across the lake overpass. The bridge is low enough to give you a close look at the lake and high enough to provide good views in all directions. On descending to paths skirting the lagoon, new vistas opened before me, and my attention was drawn lakeside to the weeping willows with their graceful drooping branches swaying in the light wind. Among trees, a lakeside willow is so different in shape that it always seems to attract attention. I interrupted my walk and repaired to a park bench, where I sat motionless, yielding to the motion to people passing by and the movement of the lake and the swan boats gently swaying at their moorings near the bridge.

There are few creations of nature that are as graceful and statuesque as a hardwood tree. There is no man-made monument that can rival the beauty of a tree or the powerful visual impression it creates—those were my feelings as I walked through the grove of trees in the Public Garden. Those trees come from around the world, and many have an ornamental character. Each is labeled, providing its common name and botanical appellation. Those trees were a gift of Harvard University and were originally raised at the Arnold Arboretum in Jamaica Plain and replanted in the Public Garden. A common feature of the trees is their hardwood character; this enables them to survive the Boston winters, which tend to be subdued in that locale because of its proximity to the harbor, the bay, and the Charles River. There are wonderful specimens of standard hardwood trees, including oak, elm, linden, beech, and maple, in addition to ornamentals such as the pagoda tree. The trees in the Public Garden convey a sense of beauty and isolation.

Most trees appear most comfortable in their own habitat and with other, similar trees close by. Hence, transplanting trees to a different part of the world and presenting them in isolation detracts from the impression. The feeling toward many of the trees in the park is that they are like a collection of assorted types, often two of this and two of that. Trees in their natural habitat for me are more interesting. In a way, an isolated tree is like a deer separated from the herd—there is always something missing on seeing the individual animal outside its social environment in nature.

In the Public Garden the trees often have unique characters—various elements may be distinctive. Those include the silhouette and height of the tree, the branches and the trunks, and the bark and the leaves. The leaves of hardwood trees have different shapes, but there is some overlap in form. I like the stately tall English oaks, which project an image of strength and character. Their leaves are fairly narrow and have prominent serrations. I like maple trees for their less imposing height and beautiful, generously proportioned, symmetrical hand-shaped leaves. The beeches are standouts, having stout trunks, thin and delicate silver-gray bark, roots that climb above ground, and branches that are very long and droop to the ground. One variety, the purple beech, has maroon leaves, and in the spring, the unusual color captures immediate attention. Ornamental trees in the park include maidenhair trees, which have uniquely shaped leaves. The presentation of such a large variety of diverse broadleaf trees in such a relatively small area is impressive.

The park extends from the Arlington Street entrance to the Charles Street exit. The Charles Street exit opens up new vistas to a much larger and irregularly shaped park fashioned by nature, the Boston Common. As spring draws to a close and summer is nigh, we turn our attention to a very different environment in which the meticulously arranged order seen in the Public Garden is replaced by an independent spirit that reigns in a hilly expanse of land that seems untouched by human hands, the Common. It is a change from the repository of social order to that of the brooding chaos that permeates the Common. The geographic proximity of these two parks is close, but the character of one is a world apart from the other, and the transition between the two is virtually nonexistent. Moreover, in moving from one park to the next, one gets the feeling that the younger, well-endowed park, the Public Garden, lacks the power to redeem the neglected one, Boston Common.

* * *

SUMMER IN BOSTON COMMON

Boston Common is a hilly natural preserve in the center of the city, bordered on the north by an even taller group of hills that coalesce to form Beacon Hill, on the south by the Boylston Street area, on the east by Downtown, and on the west by the Public Garden and Back Bay. It has a pentagonal shape and contains about fifty acres of hilly terrain, demarcated by five streets: Beacon Street on the north, Boylston Street on the south, Tremont and Park Streets on the east and Charles Street on the west. The Boylston Street side is at a low point. Moving to the interior, the elevation rises toward Beacon Street at the foot of Beacon Hill. The elevation at Charles Street is low, similar to the Public Garden, and the land slopes upward toward the center of the park and is rather steep along Beacon Street.

The Common has a very different character, depending on the street it borders. The Beacon Street side is upscale, being residential and historic. The Boylston Street side is commercial and somewhat seedy. The Charles Street side is parkland, facing the Public Garden to the west, and the Tremont Street and Park Street sides face a commercial and historic area, Downtown.

ORIGIN OF BOSTON COMMON
The retreat of the glacier in the last Ice Age left several hills in the central area of Boston, including a few that coalesce to form Beacon Hill and the other of lower elevation directly to the south, Boston Common. The glacier left the hills in its wake by moving earth and stone and also carving out the lowlands in between the hills. When it receded from the city to the north, Back Bay was left as a marsh-filled body of water about five feet deep and had a water level that rose and fell with the tides of the nearby Charles River.

A SCENE FROM AN EARLIER TIME
In the summer of 1476, three hundred years before the independence of our nation, a Wampanoag brave stood on a high place on a hill in the center of Boston later to be called Boston Common. He had crossed the Charles River by canoe and spent the day hunting in the hills of the peninsula. As the setting sun brought a spectacular flush of pink and red hues streaking across the sky to the west, he held his hands up to the heavens, and a song of prayer was on his lips, calling out to his tribal ancestors and invoking the grace of Kautantowwit, the Good Spirit. The stillness on the hill was pierced by the plaintive rhythmic murmurings of the brave. The scene of that era was also a view to many centuries past that had seen little change in tribal life, and there was no way to foresee the immense changes that were to come in the next two hundred years.

THE AMERICAN INDIAN CIVILIZATION
The Algonquians were a nation of Indian tribes centered mainly in Canada. From there they moved southward and also established a presence along the Great Lakes and along the northeastern coast of North America for many centuries before the arrival of the Europeans. The

New England tribes spoke a particular dialect of the Algonquian language. The Indians' social organization was tribal, and they lived in extended families. There was mobility of families among the tribes. The Algonquians were nomadic to a certain extent—they would move from one place to another to improve chances for food acquisition and for better seasonal conditions. They were an industrious people who thrived in the area by hunting, fishing, and cultivating corn, beans, and squash. They had villages with temporary dwellings that could be relocated. They would construct wigwams for use in the warm weather and wood houses for the winter. The wigwam was a tent built with a tree sapling frame and animal skin stretched around it. There was a large opening so that a fire could be maintained in the center of the tent for cooking and for heating in the winter. They stored various types of food as well. Taking advantage of the seasonality of hunting, they would concentrate their efforts on an area when the animal population was abundant. They used nets and hook and line for fishing. They navigated the rivers and coastal waterways in canoes built of birchwood. Men would hunt the larger sea animals, including whales, porpoises, walruses, and seals. Women and children would gather the sea animals that clustered at the shoreline, including scallops, clams, mussels, and crabs.

Hunting in the winter was with bow and arrow. Bows were made of curved oak, maple, or hickory branches and the strings from animal skins. Arrowheads were made of highly polished triangular stones. The braves set animal traps as well. Women and children would fashion the stone arrowheads and monitor the traps. The men hunted mostly deer, and to a lesser extent, moose, bear, turkeys and ducks.

The tribal leader, called a sachem, usually a member of a family of leaders, presided over important community matters. The tribal council members, or sagamores, would help in the evaluation of issues. The medicine man, called a shaman, presided over herbal treatments and said prayers for the sick.

The Indians in Massachusetts Bay Colony included several tribes. The Wampanoag, meaning "People of the Sunrise," or Massasoit, was the major tribal group in the Massachusetts area along the Atlantic coast, which included Cape Cod, Plymouth, Boston, and Cambridge of today. The Wampanoag peoples included the Nauset, Nantucket, Pennacook, Pokanoket, and Pocasset, and they were located in the eastern part of the colony and along the Atlantic Ocean in the area of Cape Cod. They spoke a dialect of the Algonquian language called Massachusett. The Wampanoag were concentrated in Cape Cod and the adjacent land area, and it was they who helped the Pilgrims get a foothold in the area. The Wampanoags taught the settlers their methods of planting and also introduced them to their practices of hunting and fishing. The Mohegan, comprising the Nipmuc and Pequot, were centrally located. The Mahican tribes, including the Pocumtuc, were in the Berkshires and across the border in the colony of New York.

BOSTON COMMON IN THE HANDS OF THE PURITANS

The Puritans arrived in Boston in 1630 and purchased the land, including the Common, from William Blaxton, an early European settler in the Shawmut Peninsula. Blaxton was an Anglican minister who came to Massachusetts Bay Colony in 1623 with the Gorges expedition and landed in Weymouth. In 1625, he relocated to Boston after he bought a large amount of land from the Indians. A monument at the corner of Park and Tremont Streets indicates that Boston Common was established in 1634 after the Puritans bought the land from Blaxton, and planned to use it as a training field but it notes that it was also used for cattle grazing.

The early settlers built dwellings mostly in the downtown area and in the North End, not far from the harbor. For some reason, the Common was never used for building purposes. One explanation might be that it is a hilly and remote area—distant from the outer harbor. Another is that it was close to the marshes of Back Bay. The sign at the entrance to the park says "Boston Common 1634." That, however, is a good example of historical arrogance, as the site was in existence long before that. It was fashioned by the retreat of the glacier and had a long but mostly unknown history after that. The Common in the Shawmut Peninsula was a hunting ground for native people, and it had a long history before Blaxton, and later the Puritans, arrived. That history is mostly unknown. The arrival of the Europeans changed civilization in Massachusetts but left Boston Common mostly unchanged. It remained a rock-filled and hilly terrain with clusters of trees.

With the appearance of the European settlers, the Common was used as a cow pasture. Families with one or a few cows and farmers with large herds would bring their cattle to graze on the land. The early settlers also used the Common for public executions until 1817. The martyrs of Puritan ecclesiastical law were executed there, including those professing different religious beliefs and those accused of witchcraft. In 1713 there was rioting at the site by two hundred citizens over food shortages, and the lieutenant governor was shot during the riot. The Common was used as a military camp by the British during the period of their military occupation of Boston from 1768 to 1776. Throughout its history, the Common has been a place for public demonstrations, often reflecting social and political discontent, and it has also witnessed unsavory diatribes by demagogues on various matters.

BOSTON COMMON AS A PUBLIC PARK

The role of the Common as a public park came about around 1830 when cattle were banished from the site, ending the two-hundred-year period of domestic animal grazing on the land. An ornamental wrought-iron fence was erected around the perimeter, but over the subsequent years little else was done to enhance its appearance. The Common was designated as a park, but overall there was little change, and even to this day it has the appearance of a natural preserve. Boston Common is an original landscape and because it has not changed much over its history, we can call it an honorary park. It does, however, have a token amount of man-made elements such as walking paths and streetlamps. Nevertheless, it has all the limitations and challenges of the original landscape. It is difficult to explain why the park still has a rough and unpolished character, but change is always possible.

ON A CLEAR DAY

One of the interesting issues is the impression of the park on entering from different locations. The impression is different since each entrance has a distinct appearance and character, and the park is so large and unstructured. The Boylston side has the Central Burying Ground; the Beacon Street side has the Frog Pond and leads to the State House. Beacon Street, adjacent to the Common, is the border street with the most historical character and beauty. Anyone who has spent time on the Common will tend to be attracted to the high ground of Beacon Street on the southern slope of Beacon Hill. When the Puritans founded Boston, it was mostly the flat land near the harbor on which the settlers built. That was in Downtown and the North End of today.

There were a number of manor homes along the southern slope of Beacon Hill, including that of the Hancock family, but the hill itself was not settled at the time. It was only in the early 1800s that Beacon Hill saw residential development, much of it inspired by the architect Charles Bulfinch, who had designed the new State House, built on Beacon Street in 1798, which was the replacement for the old State House on State Street. It is a street that from its intersection with Charles Street moves up- and downhill where it empties into Tremont

Street. The State House is built on a hill. The ascent of Beacon Street from Charles Street up to the State House is rather steep, and then there is the equally steep descent into Tremont Street.

It seems that most of the visitors in the Common tend to cluster around focal points at its periphery in two major areas. The two main areas of attraction in the park are the Beacon Street side, which presents the State House and other Beacon Hill buildings, and the Park Street side, where the T station and Brewer Fountain are located. It is from those peripheral locations that they have ready access to bordering streets. There is much less entry into the interior, which tends to have sites of only occasional use such as the bandstand. If you walk through the center of the park, which is rather isolated, you realize that there are very few people around. That could change if the park had a thorough makeover.

BEACON HILL

Beacon Hill at the time of the bicentennial of our independence was a small community that had no more than about ten thousand residents. The historic character of the neighborhood is reflected in the narrow streets and the buildings which are low in height and are very close one to another. It is like an island in history. Its borders are sharply demarcated and the character of the neighborhood is lost abruptly at its northern slope as Cambridge Street winds around it and heads for the Longfellow Bridge.

William Blaxton chose the southern slope of Beacon Hill to build the family home and plant an orchard. Beacon Hill consisted of three hills: Mount Vernon, Mount Pemberton, and Beacon Hill. Those hills were present at the time of the initial European settlement in the area. In the late 1700s, the smaller hills were razed to the ground and Beacon Hill was lowered by about 50 feet in the construction of the new State House.

Beacon Street originated mostly as a tree-lined cow path. In the early days after the establishment of the town of Boston in 1630, the residents built a mast sixty-five feet high with a tar bucket at the top that could be lit if there was a threat to the city. At that time, the southern slope of Beacon Hill abutted on Boston Common—there was no street to handle traffic except the extension of School Street, which reached up into Beacon Hill. Access to the southern slope of Beacon Hill was from the north via George Street, which intersected with Cambridge Street. Beacon Street subsequently replaced the cow path and was constructed after the revolutionary war at about the time the new State House was built. When Back Bay was filled in, Beacon Street continued its move to the west along with the development of the settlement. When Brookline was settled, Beacon Street continued westward through the town and found its way into the outermost reaches of Newton, where it merged with Washington Street and continued as Washington Street into Wellesley.

The State House was built in 1798 on land that John Hancock inherited from his uncle and aunt. The Hancock home was an adjacent property and the site that the State House is built on measures close to seven acres and served as a grazing meadow for the Hancock family's livestock. The architect Charles Bulfinch modeled the structure after buildings of similar style in London.

The architectural style is Federal, with a brick front featuring a projecting central rectangular element, which includes a portico, with seven tall tablet-shaped doorways on the first floor, and twelve white columns with Corinthian capitals on the second floor; the outside four on each side are paired, and those more centrally located are individual columns. The columns enclose large recessed rectangular windows. The third floor has a house-shaped pediment, and behind that is a large dome that has a gilded copper surface giving it a golden appearance. Atop the dome is a towerlike structure that has the appearance of a finial. It has a similar style to the one atop the old State House. In the recessed portion of the facade on each side are three large rectangular windows on the first floor and three large tablet-shaped windows on the second floor. Properly proportioned stone stairs rise from the street level to the building's entrance, with a few landings intervening. Wrought iron handrails are present on either end of the stairs. Statuary is present on the front grounds and the property is enclosed by a wrought-iron fence that sits on a concrete base that runs the length of the front border of the property.

The State House is built on a hill, and its ground level is high above the street level. The ascent to the first floor seems to be the equivalent of more than one story of the building itself. The building features a pleasing blend of the red brick color and the white color of the columns and windows. The presentation emphasizes the frontal aspect, which immediately captures attention from various vantage points—there is little else one can appreciate from a distance as the structure is at the top of a hill and there are neighboring structures on either side. In that respect it seems very different from its predecessor, much of whose architectural charm derived from its form in three dimensions. The sidewalk along Beacon Street tends to be very narrow, especially at the entrance to the State House grounds and along the descent of Beacon Street.

The State House faces Boston Common, and the part of the Common near Beacon Street is relatively flat. As noted earlier that part of the Common was used for grazing cows. For most residents of Beacon Hill, the edge of the Common is the major public park area. The Common is at their doorstep, so to speak, while the Public Garden is not exactly close by and more convenient to Back Bay residents. The Beacon Street side of the Common, adjacent to a historic residential area and the State House, gives the impression of being better preserved and maintained than many other areas of the Common.

It is ironic and lamentable that Hancock's home at 30 Beacon Street was not preserved. It is said that Hancock wanted to will the property to the Commonwealth, but for one reason or another that never happened. The state bought the property for a nominal price but was unable to get the backing to refurbish it. It owned the property at a time when there was little thought given to the preservation of historic places. Also, there was misguided state political wrangling among communities outside Boston about preserving a Boston political leader's home. It has also been noted that at the time there was a resurgence of loyalist sentiment among the legislators who didn't want to be identified with the revolutionaries. The demise of Hancock's home was a great loss for the Commonwealth as the home had a long and honorable history and was associated with an American patriot and governor of Massachusetts.

An additional anecdote of Beacon Hill history involved two residents of the neighborhood. One Sunday morning, Kevin White, mayor of Boston, who resided in Beacon Hill, was running in the Common and witnessed a purse snatching. The thief grabbed the purse of woman who was sitting on a park bench. The mayor, a Boston Marathon runner, gave chase, and the thief dropped the purse in flight. Mr. White picked it up and returned it to the distraught woman. He then summoned some police officers to chase the thief and apprehend him. This inspiring story of civic pride, actually a politician's public relations dream story, found its way into the *Boston Globe*.

BOSTON COMMON, A NATURAL HABITAT FOR BIRDS

In the summer, New England is host to many migratory birds. Small birds arrive in the early spring, if the weather is favorable, and leave in the fall before the harsh winter takes hold. In March, the larks, eastern phoebes, and swallows appear. In April, warblers and sparrows can be seen, and it is not till May that other birds arrive, including the yellow throats, kingfishers, thrushes, rose-breasted grosbeaks and the ruby-throated hummingbirds. Those birds visit the Common in the warm weather and leave as fall sets in. The colorful birds often take refuge in the tree branches and are not often viewed. Their calls signal their presence nearby, and they often visit in pairs. The daytime city noises in the adjacent streets make identifying the calls a great challenge. But early in the morning before the din, or later when it subsides, the birds can be identified by their unique calls.

The Common is very close to the harbor, so harbor birds make regular visits, including the cormorants who visit water ponds, natural or man-made. The cormorants come from the harbor, and whenever I would see one in the Common, I would think that it was the same one I would see at Rowe's Wharf. But I could not be sure because at the wharf I could only catch a glimpse of it perched on wooden docking columns several hundred feet away in the harbor. Seagulls are also frequently seen in the Common and Downtown. A visit by Canada geese in the late summer is a frequent event. They begin their southward migration about that time, and they fly in a V formation at an altitude of about three thousand feet. They can easily be seen in flight from the ground. Loons and swans favor the lakes and small ponds, as do ducks and geese. I have observed different types of aquatic birds in the collecting pools of small fountains. However, the larger birds are much less frequently seen compared with the smaller birds. Among the latter are birds that are most comfortable in the bush such as the songbirds and others that are domesticated city birds which are very comfortable on the city sidewalks such as the European starlings, house sparrows, robins, grackles, crows, and pigeons. The smaller birds are ever-present visitors on the sidewalks and near benches at the edge of the park. They tend to be domesticated and are not disturbed by the presence of people.

One day I was walking along the interior of the Common, not very far from Tremont Street, and I noticed that a small bird had fallen. Not far from the walking path and several feet away stood a bird that I recognized as a bird of prey, a peregrine falcon. The falcon had a blue-gray back, a mottled black-and-white underbelly and a black head with an aquiline face. It was about the size of a small owl and was a rare and unexpected visitor to the park. There was a tinge of yellow near the beak and around its neck. The bird standing motionless attracted the attention of quite a few people, who were astounded by the scene that had unfolded before they arrived. The presence of a predatory bird in a city park with its victim close by brought to light an occurrence that is frequent in nature but rarely seen in the human environment. Someone familiar with the bird mentioned that it had perching sites on the ledges of certain buildings at the edge of Beacon Hill from where it launched its aerial attacks on other birds. The peregrine falcon, also called a duck hawk, is a bird-hunting descendant of the raptors, which can reach a maximum flight speed of about 240 miles per hour, making it the fastest bird on earth. Its wingspan of forty-two inches is about twice the size of the bird's total length. It is prevalent in the northeastern part of North America.

AT THE CORNER OF TREMONT AND PARK STREETS

I walked from there in the direction of Tremont Street toward the northeastern corner of the park. At the corner of Tremont and Park Streets there are two rather disparate elements in the Common. Very near the Park Street corner is a one-story stone building enclosure over the Park Street T station that looks like a house, and not more than a hundred feet to the south is Brewer Fountain.

The T station at that location is in the inbound direction. The Green Line, which brings passengers all the way from the outreaches of Newton adjacent to Route 128 and from various parts of Brookline to the downtown area, lets out in Boston Common in Park Street Station.

The size of the building over the T when compared with the size of nearby buildings gives the deceptive impression that there is little activity associated with the T station. Actually, during rush hour there is a large stream of commuters that comes out of that station and disperses throughout the city streets to various work destinations. Anyone from Newton or Brookline who comes by the T is familiar with the northeast corner of the park, which features an outdoor fountain called Brewer Fountain very close by.

Brewer Fountain is a bronze work of art that was cast in Paris and presented as a gift to the city by Gardner Brewer in 1868. Brewer ordered the fountain to be shipped from Switzerland and kept it in the backyard of his home in Beacon Hill before giving it as a gift to the city of Boston. The fountain is a copy of an original work by Jean Liénard, which was featured at the World's Fair in Paris in 1855. At the base are figures of Neptune, the god of the oceans and seas; his wife, Amphitrite; Acis, a young man; and Galatea, the sea nymph he fell in love with, all characters from Greek mythology. At the second tier in the sculpture are figures of young boys backing up against a column that holds a water lily topped by a finial. The fountain reaches twenty-two feet in height and weighs fifteen thousand pounds. It is mostly a sculpture with a scant fountain element to it. When the fountain is working, small jets of water flow from narrow spouts in the sculpture from above and also from gargoyle images near the principal figures, and there are thin streams of water in motion with very little accumulating in the concrete fountain basin below. It is without any doubt a very attractive work of art, but it's a most incongruous element in Boston Common. I say this because the Common was in the grips of the Puritans for two hundred years, and the city of Boston has a heavy English influence. So a French work of art of the modern era in that location is an anomaly. It will be recalled that Manet's work, *Le Déjeuner sur l'Herbe*, was first exhibited in 1863 at the Salon des Refuses and caused quite an upheaval in art, introducing nudity in painting with powerful emphasis created by the placement of the nude subject as a very isolated but central element in the picture. The depiction of the topless mythological women in Brewer Fountain is perhaps less of an upheaval in art, but it is unparalleled in Boston, and it was placed there in the Victorian era.

In the summer heat, Brewer Fountain is like a mirage of an oasis in a desert. The summer city air is quite oppressive in that area which is paved with much concrete and abuts Downtown. The languid air is prone to being unmovable, as the surrounding buildings tend to block the breezes, so the air stagnates. The fountain is a curiosity in many ways, certainly with respect to its location in the park. One can say that it has a captive audience, in that anyone who exits the T Station and heads south will see it. It generally attracts considerable interest as reflected the number of people sitting in the area. It seems to serve as a magnet for people with an inner romantic spirit. There are devotees of the work who seem to visit frequently, attracted by its frankness and beauty. Conversely, there are likely people who will shy away from the fountain because of its presentation. Among those are people who would be uncomfortable sitting close to the fountain preferring rather to gaze on it from a distance. Some people appear attracted to the nautical theme and Boston, being a port city, has a very strong historical connection with seafaring in the Atlantic Ocean and beyond.

There was one man I noted who was a regular visitor to the site. He wore a bandanna wrapped around his head and had decorative earrings in both ears. He wore a T-shirt with horizontal red stripes and pants that seemed like tight breeches. If I were to guess his professional identity, I would say he could be an actor portraying a pirate ship's mate of the early 1700s. Another regular visitor walked with a wobbly gait and carried a bottle of whiskey in a brown paper bag and would sit not far from the fountain. He didn't say much and would find a seat on a park bench.

The fountain is a great artistic addition to the austere Common. It lifts the spirits of the Park in many ways. From Brewer Fountain there are interesting vistas to be seen particularly in the direction of Beacon Hill. Along one wide pathway that ascends to Beacon Street, the State House can be clearly seen overlooking the Common.

As you walk down the Tremont Street border of the Common you draw closer to the Boylston Street intersection. Along the Common, Tremont Street of today was called Common Street, but beyond School Street, it was called Treamount Street, a name which connotes the three hills of its Beacon Hill neighbor. Boylston Street was called Frog Lane. At that intersection there is the Boylston T station which services the area. Heading east, Boylston becomes Essex Street just beyond Washington Street, which leads to Chinatown and the Leather District.

At that time of the bicentennial, there was a homeless shelter Downtown, between Boylston Street and Washington Streets, near Chinatown. The homeless people would come and go, and in the mornings, there was generally a line of people waiting to get into the shelter, which opened its doors early. The homeless population would also visit the Common, and one day I was walking in the Common near the Boylston Street intersection and saw a frail-looking woman who seemed homeless, walking toward me. She was slightly ill-kempt. She asked, "Could you give me a dollar?" I gave her a dollar. I waited to see whether there was anything else she needed or wanted to say. But there wasn't. She thanked me and went on her way.

The homeless population in Boston was composed of individuals who had gotten off track for a variety of reasons. Some had mental illness, and therefore could not work. Moreover, there was the trend to deinstitutionalize patients with mental illnesses, which removed them from a sheltered environment and placed them in the general environment, where they often were not accepted. It would be difficult for them to find work, and most of the work they found did not involve much interaction with people. In addition, there were people with various addictions who could not sustain gainful employment because of that. Alcoholism and drug addiction were major problems that drove these individuals to street life. Some of those persons were veterans with post-traumatic stress disorder related to wartime experiences. There was also a population of abused spouses who had to leave home and required temporary housing in a shelter. There tends to be a high incidence of domestic and interpersonal violence associated with alcoholism and other addictions.

Along the Boylston Street border of the Common one encountered less pedestrian traffic. There were a number of stores on Boylston facing the Common that were respectable, including a music store and a concert piano vendor but there was little pedestrian traffic on that street, likely due to the neighborhood, which had rough edges to it, so to speak. The Common near Boylston Street is the site of the Central Burying Ground, and the park baseball field and bandstand are situated on the Boylston side inside the park. The neighborhood near the Boylston Street side of the park and to the east of it bring to mind certain obstructive forces that have delayed development in the area. The two principal problems may be compared to the ancient scourges at sea, Scylla and Charybdis.

SCYLLA: HISTORICAL SITE PRESERVATION WITHOUT RESTORATION

There are good reasons to preserve a historical site. In many ways it involves extra effort and care. But if the objective merits that approach, it involves time and money well spent. However, simply because a site is old doesn't necessarily call for preservation. For example, it may be in poor repair, or it may be beyond repair, so consideration must be given to both its current state and its restoration potential.

The physical state of the Common is in widespread disrepair. Park benches have missing slats and are extremely worn; the concrete of the walkways often is crumbling. In addition, the park has an unkempt appearance. The shrubs and trees were not well maintained, and while it is true that full foliage tends to conceal the poor condition of the trees, when the leaves fall, the true state of the trees is revealed. They require pruning and other maintenance. The appearance of the park today is the result of years of neglect, but it has great potential.

It is difficult to refute the impression that the park seems desperately in need of rejuvenation and a better public image. Perhaps the difficulty is changing a site that has such an early origin in the history of the country, as it dates back to the founding of Boston in the 1630s. There seems to be great reluctance to alter anything that has a long history associated with it. Conservation of a historical site doesn't mean in any shape, especially if the property is in poor repair. Preservation for its own sake is not a proper excuse to withhold the money and energy required to bring a park up to date.

Another reason that makes the park almost untouchable from a political standpoint is its gruesome history along with many negatives and so few positives. The park would benefit from having a makeover, including new tree plantings and new fences. An infusion of botanicals would help bring the Common back as well. It is not enough to have monuments in the park or interesting buildings on streets near the Common, nor is much added by having the Public Garden close by. The monuments are generally in good shape, and as a general rule they require very little maintenance. The Common is much larger than the Public Garden, and it has its own needs. The problems of the Common can't be solved in the Public Garden or in the neighborhoods that surround the Common such as Beacon Hill and Downtown.

Preservation of the Common as a historic site is an important objective. But preservation is not a license to leave the site in disrepair. The city has to develop a plan to improve the Common. It was once a cow pasture, but since the cows left, not enough has been done to turn the place around. Old is not necessarily shabby, but it became that way because not enough attention was paid to it. There could be more interesting trees, higher-quality trees; there are greater possibilities than to be left in a state of neglect. There is no benefit to the city to preserve shabbiness. The Common should be spruced up with more than just a sprinkling of monuments. It has great potential. The Common is the first park in the Emerald Necklace of parks in Boston and Brookline. Upgrading the park would change it from a blemished stone in the necklace to sparkling one.

It is the responsibility of the city of Boston to upgrade the park, and it could do so with public and private backing. A well-constructed park will save money in the long run as the fundamental infrastructure is there. Be prepared to move rocks and dirt. That was done when the State House was built on Beacon Hill. It was done when the Public Garden was built. It certainly can be done with the Common and would be a worthy project.

It is often said that the first step to solving a problem is the recognition that the problem exists. It would take a certain degree of community understanding and activism on the part of the city government to embark on a project to update the Common. It would require imagination and resolve to tackle that type of problem. The political wisdom might be that there is no need to change the park—but that is the wrong attitude. It's a city park that should be a source of great pride for all. I would say that it is a rare leader in city government who would want to get involved. The Common has no political constituency. Beacon Hill, its closest neighbor, is extremely small and politically weak, so unless the voters place a high emphasis on innovative leadership, it doesn't usually come about. A leader has an agenda that includes political, social and business matters. That leader tries to address important issues outside the realm of politics. That would include dealing with social and urban blight and promoting quality education and other initiatives for the common good.

CHARYBDIS: POLITICAL STAGNATION

Political stagnation is probably the best explanation why so little has been done to upgrade the Common over the past two hundred years. Granting the Common national landmark status likely worsened the situation as it may be misinterpreted as a signal that its current status is acceptable, and no change is required. The problem of urban and social blight is a common one and the city, no stranger to it, has done little about it. Part of the lack of attention to the matter appears to be political. When one party holds power for a very long time, with unlimited terms in office and paternalism as a methodology, constituencies bloom like the flowers in spring, and there is very little opportunity for innovation in governance. Political agendas tend to be parochial and sectarian, and there is lack of leadership in many important areas. So, the popular bread and circuses and other puerile distractions tend to get the most emphasis. The spinmeisters of political correctness tend to grab attention with a prescription for inexpensive platitudes rather than more substantive investments in society. Inattention to social and urban blight tends to be a major political blind spot. The attitude that those problems are an inevitable part of the human condition should be rejected with both hands. Acquiescence with the worst in the human condition, including social anomie, is of course unacceptable. The inattention to the Common is similar to the lack of attention in Chinatown and the Leather District. It was not that the area is very large or difficult to upgrade. Clearing urban blight should be a high priority in city hall and marginal urban areas should be upgraded.

With that goal in mind, there was no good reason to locate a homeless shelter in a neighborhood bordering on Downtown. That further marginalized the area, bringing homeless people into the Common. It is not that the homeless population doesn't need shelter and recreation, but civic pride is the overriding issue here, not social welfare. The Common has to be a center of public civic pride—it should not project a negative image. The Common should be a park that adults and children can enjoy. Leaving a bordering neighborhood in poor repair and encouraging marginalization of the area is an example of poor civic planning. The area bordering on Chinatown and the Common needed upgrading, but instead it was further marginalized by placing a homeless shelter there.

Fortunately, at the time of the bicentennial of our independence, with an enlightened approach the good and bad memories of the past were soon destined to yield to rebuilding in the present, bringing hope for the future.

SUMMER IN DOWNTOWN BOSTON

DOWNTOWN BOSTON

If you were to go to downtown in any city in North America, you would be heading for the business district. Downtown is a term that originally was used in reference to the town at the southern tip of Manhattan, which developed from its first settlement on the island in 1625. That was the site of a very important business transaction in our nation's history, the purchase of Manhattan Island by Peter Minuet from the native Indians for sixty guilder, or twenty-four dollars, and trinkets.

The most common use of the term is as a business center, but other meanings have developed. Downtown often is the site where there is a concentration of entertainment such as movies, theater, and dining out. It is also a place for shopping, often upscale. Downtown may also be the site of city, state, and federal agencies that operate in the area and provide information to the public. In each city, the downtown area has particular characteristics that distinguish one place from another, and there is a wide variety of downtowns. In many places, downtown is strictly a business area, but some have also acquired residential buildings. People who make an occasional trip downtown mostly visit specific locations and barely notice the general character of the area. They come and go, often without much appreciation of the area beyond the address they visited and the business that was transacted.

In sending people to visit Downtown, I feel that it is important to let them know what to look for and to prepare them for the experience. Downtown Boston is a center of business and government. It has very little entertainment—no movie or live performance theaters, few restaurants, no museums, and only limited shopping. A walk through Downtown is certainly a walk through the business hub of the city, but it is much more than that. It is a walk through history and along streets that contain magnificent examples of various styles of building architecture from various periods in our country's history beginning in the early 1700s and continuing to the present.

DOWNTOWN NEIGHBORHOODS AND STREETS

Downtown Boston occupies a very small area and is shaped like a hand with widely outstretched fingers. Given the smallness of the area, you get the feeling that you could almost put it into your back pocket. The main area of interest is not larger than the Common. The area is divided into various sections that form a central area, including Downtown Crossing in the west, the Financial District in the east, Chinatown in the south, and Government Center in the north. It is adjacent to the more peripheral regions including the harbor, the North End, and the West End, which includes Beacon Hill. It runs from Winter and Summer Streets in a southeasterly direction down to High Street, where it continues to the north on Congress Street past Government Center to Sudbury Street and then turns in a southwesterly direction to Cambridge Street, which loops to the south, continues back to Tremont Street, and brings you back to Winter Street. The major architectural and historical attractions are enclosed by that perimeter. Another area of roughly similar size lies to the east of Congress Street. Its eastern border is Interstate 93, which makes a lazy curve toward the south as it moves through the downtown area. Beyond I-93 is the North End, a third area in Downtown Boston, which has a fairly round appearance on the map, containing wharves at its edges, appearing like finger-like extensions into Boston Harbor.

HISTORY AND ARCHITECTURE: HIGHLIGHTS OF DOWNTOWN BOSTON

Downtown Boston is a rejuvenation and modernization of history, with old and new side by side in the same scene. Downtown Boston brings out the creative spirit in the person, and a visit there is a multidimensional adventure. A complex interaction of emotions, visual stimuli, and historical meaning gives rise to a powerful impression. The impact of the scene traces to the way the buildings interact from an aesthetic point of view and the way the person feels in the environment. In addition it derives from the profound historical significance of certain places that grabs you, body and soul, and from the perspective of history, what is not seen can be even more important than what is seen.

One always has to be ready to view the unexpected. Architectural patterns are often unusual. There may be a distance of about three centuries between two buildings that are physically separated by no more than fifty feet. In general, the height of the older buildings is moderate and that of the newer buildings, including skyscrapers, is also not so high as to seem unmanageable from a visual standpoint. Excessive height tends to create a feeling of alienation in the viewer. The smaller and more tortuous the streets, the lower the height of the buildings that can be accommodated from a visual perspective. Moreover, the taller the building, the greater the challenge is to make it aesthetically pleasing and balanced.

To obtain a more focused experience, explore the area on foot and always bring a compass. You may be heading east at the moment, but in a minute or so, you could be heading north or south. Downtown Boston streets often meander from one direction to another. If you are standing at the corner of Tremont and Winter Streets, my advice is this: go east down Winter Street but don't dally in Downtown Crossing. Just keep going east, and you will find things worth looking at. Going south is a journey into a red-light district; going north is a trip to city hall; and going west puts you in the wrong direction, back to the Common.

In Downtown, if you just walk without paying attention to the street names you might walk an hour and come back to the place where you started. You always come back to the starting place at some point because of the circularity of the streets, as long as you don't cross a very major thoroughfare. A good example is Milk Street, which is circular and meandering. So, if you get lost, just keep walking and if you started in the east, take a look at the compass and head in that direction to return to where you started.

Remember that the streets tend to be narrow and circular, so if you are looking for a particular building, don't expect to see it from a few blocks away. Most often you will have to make a turn, and only then will it come into view. The buildings do not necessarily face in the directions of the compass, and you might find a building or two that occupy an entire street. In olden days it was customary to construct buildings on gores, which are fragments of lots, particularly in the city center where land is limited and prices for land are high. Often that practice would lead to the construction of buildings of unusual shapes—for example, long and very narrow.

BOSTON HARBOR

Walking in downtown Boston, you can often feel the dampness and cool breezes of the harbor, but the harbor itself is nowhere in sight until you reach the wharves. That's because the area is very flat and the streets wind a lot, and with the tall buildings there is not a street-level view of the harbor. Within the city, you have to view the harbor from at least the thirteenth story of a building to capture good views. If you visited One Beacon Place at about that level and were facing the northeast, you would see the harbor very well. In the distance you would catch a glimpse of the three masts of *Old Ironsides*, the undefeated heavy frigate USS *Constitution*, in its mooring at Pier 1 in Charlestown Navy Yard across the way from the harbor.

A WALK THROUGH HISTORY STARTS WITH THE UNSEEN: THE FIRST SETTLEMENT IN MASSACHUSETTS

The original European settlement in Massachusetts was established in Plymouth in 1620 by the English immigrants. The settlers, called Pilgrims, were Protestant religious separatists who came into conflict with the Church of England. They had the same Calvinistic theology as the nonseparatist Puritans, but they could not reconcile any participation in the Anglican Church. At the time, Britain was a cauldron of Christian religious conflict due to the Protestant Reformation. Newer reformist theologies were in conflict with Anglican traditions in a fierce religious ideological battle. The Crown was at the head of the Church of England and various separatists, including the Pilgrims, were persecuted and sought refuge elsewhere in Europe.

So they left for Holland, where they found religious tolerance and some work, but they had austere lives. They found it difficult to live in the midst of a foreign culture and were concerned about the weakening of their religious autonomy in the presence of the foreign influence. Most important, they needed more economic opportunities. They decided to relocate to the New World, hoping to find better living conditions and prosperity and greater opportunity to promote their English heritage according to their own religious philosophy and practice. A small number of the members of the congregation from Leiden, Holland, came on the Mayflower and eventually landed in Plymouth and established a settlement called Plimoth Plantation. They endured many tribulations in their maiden voyage at sea; they were stricken with smallpox, and only forty-seven colonists survived the diseases they contracted on the ship. Only about half of the crew of the Mayflower survived the voyage. They led a simple life centered on their religious principles, and they had good relations with the neighboring Indians, who taught them agricultural methods they practiced in the area.

THE SECOND SETTLEMENT IN NEW ENGLAND WAS IN BOSTON BY THE PURITANS

The town of Boston was founded in 1630 by Puritan settlers from England. Two years earlier they had signed an agreement with England, granting them the right to establish the Massachusetts Bay Colony, a self-governing entity in the New World. John Winthrop was their leader. The settlers arrived at a place north of Boston, the city of Salem of today, but they were forced to move southward because of lack of food. They relocated to Charlestown but had to move from there because of inadequate fresh water. They were introduced to a nearby area to the south by the first English settler in the area, William Blaxton. If ever there was an intrepid pioneer in the history of the new world, it was he. He settled with his family on the Shawmut Peninsula, and they were the only residents there at the time. He came to the area in 1625 and built a house and an orchard at the corner of Beacon and Spruce Streets. The friendly Wampanoags were on the other side of the Charles.

The Puritans favored that site, present-day Boston, and bought the land from Blaxton. The Puritans, being nonseparatists, had more political and financial support in England. The Puritans were industrious and prospered, largely through trade with England. The society they established emphasized religious obligations and practice together with education. One of their early initiatives was the establishment of Harvard College in 1636.

In Boston there are no buildings that survive from the 1600s as they were made of wood and held up poorly in the damp environment adjacent to the harbor. The only structures that survive from that era are the wharves that project into the harbor. The buildings were replaced by brick structures in the early 1700s once brick manufacturing came into being.

A WALK BACK INTO AMERICAN HISTORY ON THE ROAD TO AMERICAN INDEPENDENCE

In the decade starting in 1760, there was no place in the United States closer to the center of the economic tensions and political conflicts between the thirteen colonies and Britain than the town of Boston. Its harbor was a gateway of trade to the New World. Its port of Boston served the entire Northeast as a major center of commerce between Britain and the colonies. Through that port, English manufactured goods came to the colonies and wheat, fish, tobacco, and other commodities were sent to Britain. As unfair tariffs and trade restriction were points of contention, it is not surprising, therefore, that Boston was a major focal point in the breakdown of relations between the colonies and the mother country.

Trade and political relations between the colonies and Britain before the decade of 1760 were mutually advantageous and respectful.

The trading partnership served the business needs of the principals and was the main issue, rather than taxes or tariffs. However, trade relations started to deteriorate after the French and Indian War. A period of economic recession followed the seven-year conflict, leaving Britain and the colonies in debt. For Britain the national debt swelled to about 120 million pounds. Determined to recoup some of that debt by means of taxes and tariffs, the British government levied taxes on trade to the colonies. There had been taxes and tariffs imposed earlier, but they were met by lax observance and enforcement, and avoidance through smuggling as well. For example, with respect to molasses before 1760, on average, colonial merchants were paying only about one and one-half pence per gallon in tariff, although the official rate was six pence. In the Sugar Act of 1763, Britain lowered the official tax rate on molasses from six pence per gallon to three pence per gallon and coupled it with strict enforcement. The change in the tax rate and the more zealous enforcement effectively doubled the amount of tax that was due. They also prohibited importation of rum to the colonies; this was a maneuver that had broader ramifications. Molasses, a major English export item from the West Indies, was used in the production of rum; therefore, prohibiting the importation of rum was a way to promote the importation of molasses. In addition, taxes were imposed on additional items including hides, skins, potash, logwood, and other goods.

As far as tariffs were concerned, infractions of various sorts were adjudicated by the British naval court in Halifax. It was said that in all cases heard regarding tariff matters, the court held a presumption of guilt rather than innocence. That presumption reflected the reality of the times as tariff avoidance was very common. Notwithstanding that reality, the approach was a disadvantage to the accused, and that incensed the ship owners and captains, who were brought before the court and evoked the sympathy of the colonists, who viewed the tariffs as an unfair economic burden and an obstacle to trade.

A Chronological Summary of Taxes and Trade Restrictions by Britain on the American Colonies during the Decade prior to the American Revolution

Year	Act	Provisions
1763	Acts of 1763	a. Established standing armies in the colonies
		b. Prohibited settlement west of Appalachian Mountains
1764	Currency Act	a. Required that colonial debt be paid in British currency
		b. Blocked the colonies from issuing their own paper currency
1764	Sugar Act	Imposed tariff on molasses
1765	Stamp Act	Compelled use of tax stamp on official documents and playing cards
1765	Quartering Act	Forced colonists to pay for housing British troops
1767	Townshend Acts	Imposed duties on tea, paper, lead, paint imported into colonies; repealed in 1770
1773	Tea Acts	Created regulations and a tea duty that favored the East India Company, which had a surplus of 17 million pounds of tea
1774	Coercive and Intolerable Acts	
	Boston Port Act	Closed the port of Boston
	Massachusetts Government Act	Rewrote Massachusetts Charter to replace elected with royally appointed officials and restricted town meetings
	Administration of Justice Act	Provided for extradition of colonists accused of crimes to other colonies or Britain for trial

    The laws imposing financial levies on the colonists and restricting their economic opportunities were regarded as provocations. In reaction to those provocations, colonists took various measures.

TAX LEVIES AND RESTRICTIONS OF TRADE

Important sources of resentment in the colonies to English governance were taxes, tariffs, and trade restrictions. The taxes and tariffs applied to various agricultural and industrial products and came at a time of economic recession. The colonists objected because they felt they were burdensome, unjust, and unnecessary. Moreover, they objected in principle, as well, because they had not given their consent to the levies. In addition, the taxes were referred to as external taxes, in the sense that they did not support the colonies. The trade restrictions had various dimensions. First, there was a prohibition of manufacturing items that were produced in Britain and exported to the colonies. Then, there was a limitation in importation of rum, which favored the importation of molasses used for making the rum. Then, in 1763, there was a restriction in westward migration in the New World. Westward migration beyond the Appalachian Mountains was prohibited, and the control of the west was retained by Indian tribes. Opportunity was in the west, which was rich in natural resources, and the westward migration was considered to be essential for the destiny of the colonists. The trade restrictions were an even worse threat than tariffs and taxes because they limited business opportunity and blocked the growth of the economies in the colonies. Trade restrictions were perceived as an attempt to manipulate trade in favor of Britain, and there was very pervasive noncompliance in both categories.

COLONIES' REACTIONS TO TAX LEVIES AND TRADE RESTRICTIONS

First, merchants met in various colonies and urged the colonial legislatures to object to taxation without the consent of the colonies. There was also active resistance to specific legislative acts involving taxes and tariffs through avoidance and other acts of noncompliance. There was strong opposition to the Stamp Act in Massachusetts, Connecticut, Rhode Island, New York, New Jersey, Maryland, Pennsylvania, Virginia, and Georgia. For example, in Virginia, resolutions opposing the Act were brought in the House of Burgesses by Patrick Henry. Merchants in all of the colonies vowed to boycott British goods. The anger over the Stamp Act led to the Stamp Act Congress in New York. In North Carolina, colonists seized the ports of Wilmington and Brunswick. In certain instances, the frictions led to violence, as occurred in the Boston Massacre. Multiple colonial legislatures voted for nonimportation declarations against British goods.

MAINTAINING A STANDING ARMY AND PAYING FOR QUARTERING OF BRITISH TROOPS

Another source of friction was the decision in 1763 to maintain a standing army in the colonies after the French and Indian War, and then in 1765 to compel the colonists to bear the cost of quartering troops. The political rationale provided for that decision was that it provided a means for protection of the colonies from the French and Indians, but the need for that was dubious as the French had largely been removed from the colonies, and the Indians alone were not a major threat as the colonies had their own militias. Instead, the standing military force was viewed as a means to intimidate the population in respect to tax and trade regulation compliance. There were administrators appointed by Britain; some were local, but many governed from Britain, and they had little power to enforce compliance. The presence of a military force was thought to provide assistance along those lines, but in reality that was not the situation. As a matter of principle and practice, no army in the world has the power to promote compliance in those matters. In addition, the colonies conducted business with other countries, so there were alternatives to British imports and the tariffs associated with them.

REACTIONS TO QUARTERING OF BRITISH TROOPS

In 1765, additional legislation entitled the Quartering Act made it the colonists' obligation to pay for the housing of the troops. In Boston, the resentment toward Britain was in large measure due to quartering of British troops. In that era, the downtown area of today had a residential character and was inhabited mostly by tradesmen, craftsmen, and small-business owners. The largest structures were meeting places and places of worship. The arrival of British troops in the town of Boston occurred about three years later, and from that time forward, the presence of British military in the center of town became progressively more irksome.

In that era, the town was smaller than it is today. There were marsh areas in the periphery, and the western border was the western border of the Common, which overlooked the marshes of Back Bay. Sending troops to Boston was like sending troops to London—the British had to be very cautious and circumspect in preserving the peace as the area was replete with loyalists. Since the town was small, there was no place within it where the military presence was not felt. And as a matter of principle, there was no room in the town for even one British soldier.

In the midst of the problems encountered related to the Townshend Acts and the increasingly vocal objections and demonstrations, the British sent two regiments from Halifax and six weeks later two more regiments from Ireland. In all seasons, troops were housed in the court house and Faneuil Hall; in the summer, some of the soldiers were encamped in the Common.

In the British occupation dating from 1768 to 1776, the town of Boston had a residential character, and it also served as a port city with many wharves fanning out into the harbor. The town was filled with the self-employed: tradesmen, craftsmen, and mercantilists. The tradesmen and craftsman were more self-reliant and more independent minded than the mercantilists, who depended on Britain for trade.

THE BOSTON FOUR: POLITICAL VISIONARY, SHIPPING MERCHANT, MEDICAL DOCTOR, AND SILVERSMITH

SAMUEL ADAMS, POLITICAL VISIONARY

Samuel Adams, a Boston political leader, legislator, patriot, and visionary, was a vocal opponent of the British, who by words and deeds personified the spirit of independence in the prerevolutionary period. He was an uncompromising activist whose ideas were revolutionary and who practiced what he preached. He was one of the founding fathers of the country. He was born to a merchant, Samuel Adams Sr. and his wife, Mary, in their home on Purchase Street in Boston. The family, devout Puritans, were members of the Old South Congregational Church, where his father served as a deacon.

He graduated from Harvard College in 1740 and earned a master's degree in 1743. The family's involvement in Boston politics started with his father, who served as a political functionary in various roles. As the Puritans were the first settlers in the town, they were mindful of the original contract with England, the Cambridge Agreement of 1628, which defined the relationship of the mother country and the colony and specified rights and obligations. Since that contract was signed, there had been multiple actions by England that infringed on those rights of the colonists, without their consent, and that greatly troubled him throughout his education and during his career. In prerevolutionary times, it was the contract that served as the constitution for the colonists. Each violation of the contract moved the colony farther along the road to rebellion, the gateway to independence.

In his master's thesis, he argued that resistance to the "Supreme Magistrate was lawful if the Commonwealth cannot otherwise be preserved," which clearly revealed his position. He emphasized the rights of the colonists, and he pointed out the excesses of colonialism and abuses of authority by England and its administrators.

During his career he worked tirelessly against the British rule in public and private, participating in legislative process, publishing articles, speaking at town meetings, drafting written protests, sending circular letters to other colonies to get support, and organizing demonstrations and boycotts. He was particularly incensed by the failure of the government to protect private property. Lack of respect for private property was a violation of the contract. The quartering act was an egregious breach of the government's responsibility to protect private property. He was a religious man of high moral caliber and was steadfast in his allegiance to Puritan principles in daily life. According to the Puritan way, he emphasized simplicity and virtue and rejected affectation and pretense. In 1865, he founded the Sons of Liberty, a group that eventually would be involved in the armed resistance to English rule. He was a delegate from Massachusetts to the Continental Congress in Philadelphia. Before that time, he had never set foot outside of Massachusetts. He later served as governor of the state. At the year of the bicentennial, one could say that history suggests that he merits another title: Father of American Liberty.

JOHN HANCOCK, SHIPPING MERCHANT

John Hancock was born to Reverend John Hancock and Mary Hawke Thaxter in Braintree, Massachusetts, on January 12, 1736. He was eight years old when his father died, and he was taken in by his uncle, Thomas Hancock, and aunt, Lydia Henchman Hancock, in Boston, a couple who had no children. The uncle, a wealthy shipping merchant, was the proprietor of a firm in the import and export business known as the House of Hancock. Manufactured goods would be imported from Britain, and in turn rum, whale oil, and fish were exported to Britain. Thomas was a very successful businessman, and the family prospered. They lived in a manor home on Beacon Street across from the Common at a site that is currently occupied by the Massachusetts State House.

The family had several servants and slaves who helped with household maintenance. In the early morning from the upstairs bedroom he could see the cows grazing on the Common. The Hancocks liked to entertain, and it is said that years later, when John was the master of the house, there were so many guests that they ran out of milk. The servants then rushed to the Common and milked some cows to provide for the guests with owners of the cows unaware.

John graduated from Harvard College in 1754 and as a young man spent most of his early career in Boston working for his uncle, Thomas Hancock. John was attracted to freemasonry. About one year before his uncle died in 1764, he became a partner in the firm. He subsequently inherited the family's business and assets, including the manor house on Beacon Hill.

The import-export business was very much affected by the trade restrictions and tariffs that came into effect in the middle of the decade from 1760 to 1770. Unlike in times past, the new laws were strictly enforced. In 1768, Hancock's sloop, *Liberty*, was seized by the British because of suspected smuggling. Hancock became involved in local politics and came under the tutelage of Samuel Adams, the head of the Whig party. The politics of the day favored resistance to the British and eventual revolt against their rule. Hancock called Samuel Adams the last of the Puritans, but I would say that history has proved that to be incorrect—the Puritans were a way of life, and their spirit survived in later generations, in the Brahmins, and to this day that spirit is alive and well in Boston and elsewhere in the nation.

JOSEPH WARREN, MEDICAL DOCTOR

Dr. Joseph Warren established a medical practice in the town. He graduated from Harvard College in 1759 and had four children with his wife, Elizabeth Hooten. She died in 1772, and he sent the family to stay with his sister in Worcester. He rented a home on Hanover Street in the early 1770s, where he had a clinic and devoted himself to his practice and the coming revolution. In those days, much of the general physician's work involved trauma, and victims were brought to the doctor's residence for treatment.

There was a general scarcity of doctors, and the nursing profession was in the developmental stage. Hence, nursing care was often performed by the doctor, including cleansing wounds, putting on various treatment applications, administering medicines, and monitoring a patient's progress in the home setting. The physician in those days had to be a robust walker as making patient rounds was often done on foot. It also helped for the doctor to be a good horseman, as that was the quickest means of transportation in the colonies to respond to urgent calls.

Clinical practice was based on the art and science of the day. There was much theory but little science. Thus, the practice tended to be based on treatment of symptoms. There was basic diagnosis and treatment.

Empirical treatment was often used as there was not a strong scientific basis for practice at the time. Nonetheless, empirical treatment often was successful as there was a long history of medical experience with herbals, which did help with various ailments.

PAUL REVERE, SILVERSMITH

Paul Revere, a silversmith by trade, lived nearby. He, Dr. Warren, and others were united by a fraternal bond in freemasonry and were among the Sons of Liberty, a group of local revolutionaries who dedicated themselves to the overthrow of the British regime. Paul was the son of French Huguenot father Apollos Rivoire, a silversmith who came to Boston at age eight, served as an apprentice to a local silversmith, changed his name to Revere, and married Deborah Hitchborn, whose family was established in the town and owned a shipping wharf. At the age of thirteen, Paul Revere left school to apprentice with his father. He enlisted in the provincial army in 1756 during the French and Indian War and was commissioned as a second lieutenant in an artillery regiment. He served in the army only for a short period of time and returned to Boston to work as a silversmith. He married Sarah Orne on August 4, 1757, and they had eight children. He also learned dentistry and practiced that as well.

Paul Revere had many talents. He was a master craftsman and engraver. He had many clients and developed many connections. Revere was also a physically fit person who was an excellent horseman. Revere had experience as a courier from Boston to other colonies, bringing information about the political conditions in Boston. He had military experience from his service in the provincial army. He was a friend of Dr. Joseph Warren, and they were members of the same Masonic lodges. Revere bought a house on North Square in the North End in 1770 and had his shop on Clarke's wharf. His wife, Sarah, died in 1773, and he married Rachel Walker and had eight children with her.

Revere and Warren served to guard the *Dartmouth* to prevent the unloading of the tea just before the Boston Tea Party. Revere is perhaps best known for his midnight ride to Lexington on April 18, 1775, to sound the alarm to the local residents to warn them that the British soldiers would soon arrive—and from the back of his steed he shouted, "The redcoats are coming!" The warning was also meant for Samuel Adams and John Hancock, who had relocated to Lexington because the British had ordered their arrest. That heroic ride, reflecting the firm resolve of the patriots to stand their ground, has made him a legend in American history forever.

A PICTURE OF LIFE IN COLONIAL TIMES

Life in colonial times was extremely harsh. Transportation was by foot or on horseback. Dwellings were generally small and neither well heated in the winter nor well cooled in the summer. Lighting was by candle. Women's daily routines included household chores, which were difficult. Cooking was labor intensive as raw materials had to be obtained and assembled. Preparation of a meal could take several hours. Vegetables were often homegrown. There were only primitive systems for storing perishable items in the home setting. Meats and fish were highly salted as an aid in preservation. The meals were prepared over a fire, and the main meal was served at about two o'clock in the afternoon. Bathing was only an occasional matter because the facilities were primitive.

There were two major categories of work activities in the colonies: farming and the trades on the one hand, and shipping—both import and export—on the other. Self-reliance made the farmers and tradesman more independent minded but the mercantilists were dependent on business with England. A significant proportion of the former group favored revolution, while a significant proportion of the latter group rejected it. Nevertheless, being unsympathetic to the prospect of revolution did not mean they supported the abuses of colonial power.

The notion that there were revolutionists on one side and loyalists on the other is an oversimplification. The term "loyalist" has been used too loosely—those born in the colonies had a colonial identity. They were loyal to the colonies first and to Britain second. It is foolish to think otherwise. What we call loyalty was mostly deference to authority. Also, skittishness about rebelling against Britain should not be confused with genuine loyalty. People who had recently arrived, in contrast, were different. They were transients and most would return to England. In the colonies it gradually became clear to the majority that there was no future in the status quo, which moved the country along the road to revolution and independence. Nonetheless, most of the population was preoccupied with labor-intensive daily activities, and for the average person political matters were overshadowed by the hardships.

There were other causes of friction as well, including political wrangling. On both sides there was empty rhetoric, bombast, hyperbole, pettiness, and mean-spiritedness. Taxes, tariffs, and trade restriction imposed by Britain were met with lack of compliance by the colonies. From a historical perspective, it is clear that most of the British laws were ill conceived and were consequently met with cynicism and noncompliance in the colonies. Parliament would pass acts without enough thought given to the likely unfavorable reaction to the acts. The restrictions were considered punitive, a conclusion that was inescapable, as one ill-advised tax or restriction was followed by another and yet another. As compliance was close to nil, enforcement was impossible as well. The colonies had observer status in parliament. They sent emissaries who made their positions abundantly clear. Parliament took note of the representations and repeatedly tried to provide redress. There was a significant minority in Britain that agreed with the colonists' positions.

Eventually the majority of British legislators recognized that most of the laws were not sound, and one by one they were weakened or repealed. For example, the tariffs on most of the imported items specified in the Townshend Act were mostly repealed by 1770. Nevertheless, there were major negative residuals, the most important of which was resentment over English governance. Other unresolved problems included the quartering of troops and the tea tax. The unrest in Boston prompted the British to increase in the number of troops stationed there. It was as if there was a strong premonition on both sides that violence would erupt in the not too distant future. The reaction in Boston to the quartering of troops occurred first.

BOSTON MASSACRE

With a standing militia housed in a small area such as the town of Boston, there was bound to be some conflict that would arise between the troops and the local population. The atmosphere was tense, and frictions were increasing. There was a high likelihood of a clash between the soldiers and the locals. It happened in the early part of March of 1770, when a quarrel broke out between a local rope maker, Samuel Gray, and a British officer. When a mob clashed with British soldiers, they opened fire at the mob once, killing three and wounding six others. Two of the wounded later succumbed to their injuries. The event, called the Boston Massacre, led to the withdrawal of all but one of the British regiments. They relocated to Castle William, a fort on one of the harbor islands, which was out of sight, but not far away.

BOSTON TEA PARTY: BRITISH TEA BECAME UNWELCOME IN THE AMERICAN COLONIES

Tea was subject to a tariff under the Townshend Act and even after the act was repealed, tea was still subject to a tariff. There was firm resolve in the colonies not to import English Tea and instead smuggled Dutch tea was used. The Tea Act of 1773 was passed to sell surplus tea from the East India Company. It permitted direct exportation of British tea to the colonies and reduced the tariff so that the product would be cheaper than smuggled Dutch tea. The act was met with resistance throughout the colonies as an unfair manipulation of trade.

In the early morning hours of November 28, 1773, the harbor was enveloped by a very dense fog. Gradually, the fog lifted and revealed an image in history: a New Bedford Whaler, the *Dartmouth*, loaded with British tea heading for the port and to be joined in the next three weeks by two other tea-bearing vessels, the *Eleanor* and the *Beaver*. As it approached the wharf, it encountered a premonitory apparition: the specter of tea chests rising out of the harbor and swirling about in a wild dance in the air to a chorus of voices that shouted, "No taxation without representation!" It was a foreboding of the coming tempest over tea in the town of Boston. The craft glided into the harbor and headed for Griffin's Wharf, where it docked with the objective of delivering the tea. However, Boston locals rejected that idea, suggesting instead that the tea be returned to London to the East India Company, its original owner. However, that option was blocked by the British administrator, Governor Hutchinson.

In Boston, on December 16, 1773, several thousand locals met at the Old South Meeting House to decide how to prevent the imminent unloading of the tea from the three vessels at Griffin's Wharf. The colonists wanted the tea returned to England, from where it came. However, the British administrators were blocking that option, and one ship owner, a colonist, reported that it was not possible to return the tea. So, they developed a plan to throw the tea into the harbor. Men in Mohawk Indian dress were dispatched to the wharf to throw the chests of tea into the water and a crowd of about one thousand people moved onto the wharf to shield them by blocking access. There was no resistance to what was later called the Boston Tea Party, and 342 chests of tea from the holds of the three ships were tossed into the harbor.

THE OUTBREAK OF THE AMERICAN REVOLUTION

The political atmosphere in the colonies was strained and rapidly deteriorating. The English administrators were caught in between adversaries at the center of the conflict, and their mission was both hopeless and thankless. Hopeless in the sense that it was like trying to plug leaks in a dike—no sooner was one stopped than another appeared. And thankless in the sense that neither the colonists nor the mother country were satisfied with any given approach no matter how reasonable it might be. To their great credit they fulfilled their responsibility to protect the general population. Finally, Lieutenant General Thomas Gage, commander in chief of North America, received orders from London to march on Concord to destroy the colonists' arms supply depot there.

There were a number of problems associated with that order, which would soon become apparent. First, although it had the potential of achieving its objective, destroying an arms depot also had the potential of starting an armed conflict. The British had only a token presence in Massachusetts Bay Colony—only in the port of Boston. All of the area outside of Boston was under the control of the colonists. This meant that the arms would be removed to another location if an attack was anticipated, which they were. British were unfamiliar with the area and had to depend on their own intelligence gathering, making the objective much more difficult. Also, they were very concerned about incitement of the population and loss of loyalists to their cause. Early in the morning on April 19, 1775, British troops were mobilized to the northwestern edge of Boston Common to the low waters of the Charles and crossed the river, disembarked in Cambridge, and then marched on the road to Concord. The troops were engaged on the way in Lexington by colonial minutemen, but they made their way to Concord and were also engaged there. Those events in the span of twenty-four hours ushered in the armed conflict. Once the British marched on Concord and met resistance in Lexington and then in Concord, the die was cast in favor of war. History shows that the British won those battles but in doing so set the stage for losing the war, as those battles galvanized support in the colonies for independence. And that support grew rapidly.

BATTLE OF BUNKER HILL

The Battle of Bunker Hill was the first large-scale battle of the war. The battles of Lexington and Concord by comparison were mere skirmishes. They were only chance encounters of armed patriots and British regulars. However, at Bunker Hill, the battle was planned. The events leading up to that battle were as follows. After the battles at Lexington and Concord, the patriots, who controlled the area outside of Boston, laid siege to the town, in which the British had four thousand troops. On May 25, 1775, British reinforcements arrived: forty-five hundred soldiers and three generals, Henry Clinton, William Howe, and John Burgoyne. With the British, when more senior military officers were sent, it was a signal that those of lesser rank would soon be replaced. And so it was with General Gage, who was recalled a little more than a month later, soon after the Battle of Bunker Hill.

The British planned to dislodge the colonists from their positions in the hills surrounding Boston. The British army ruled the town of Boston, the British navy ruled the harbor, and the patriots had possession of the territory outside the town. The British wanted to secure their position by capturing Bunker Hill in the north and Dorchester Heights in the south. As a first step, on June 17, 1775, they crossed the harbor and landed on the southern tip of the Charlestown Peninsula. They then marched on Bunker Hill and suffered heavy losses and casualties in the battle but managed to displace the colonists. British warships in Charlestown Harbor pounded the patriot positions, and the patriots fought fiercely and inflicted heavy casualties but they ran out of ammunition and were compelled to retreat.

On the patriot side, there were 140 dead and 310 wounded. Among the fallen was Dr. Joseph Warren, who was killed in the retreat. On the British side there were 226 dead and 828 wounded. The tenacity of the colonists in battle was a demonstration to the British that their adversary in the upcoming war was highly motivated and extremely capable. Moreover, it was also clear that the British victory at Bunker Hill was gained through an important tactical advantage, powerful warships close by in Charlestown Harbor, and that tactical advantage would be absent in most of the battles of the coming war.

EVACUATION DAY

The Second Continental Congress voted to create a Continental army on June 14, 1775, and appointed George Washington as commander in chief. One of Washington's first orders of business was the relief of Boston from British occupation. He assembled a formidable army of irregulars who took Dorchester Heights, which he fortified with heavy cannon. When that occurred, the British recognized that their position in Boston was precarious and evacuated the town on March 17, 1776.

THE SPIRIT OF RESISTANCE TO COLONIAL RULE

If there was ever a place and a time in the history of our nation in which destiny brought together valiant deeds, courageous and inspiring words, self-sacrifice in favor of the common good, and unwavering resolve to uphold basic principles of freedom and justice even if it required armed resistance, it was in Boston and the Massachusetts Bay Colony in the decade before the outbreak of the American Revolution. No written document can capture the spirit of the heroism of the people who steadfastly resisted the despotism of colonial rule. No retelling of the events of that era adequately reflects the unprecedented political upheaval that a relatively small number of people brought about. Resistance to an imperial power was virtually unprecedented. The people involved were modest in their ways, and they were not beholden to the British Crown. They had religious upbringing, and they put principles of liberty and the public good first and personal matters second. In many ways their principles and their persistence are an inspiration to all. They protested through peaceful means by the spoken or written word, expressing the outrage of the colonists over multiple violations of the colonial contract by England. The people protested through public demonstrations, legislative and other representation to the governing authorities, public speeches and writings—in all of those ways and more, the oppressed confronted the oppressors. It was only when it became clear that words were not sufficient to bring about change that people took to arms. A timeline of the resistance to British rule in Massachusetts Bay Colony is presented in the following table.

Timeline of Events in Massachusetts Bay Colony Leading to the American Revolution

Date	Event
1750	Jonathan Mayhew presents sermon at Old West Church in Boston with expression "No taxation without representation."
1761	Samuel Adams works as a reluctant tax collector and has a shortfall of 2,200 pounds.
1764	Boston merchants publish "Reasons Against Renewal of the Stamp Act."
December 17, 1765	Loyal Nine (Sons of Liberty) established to resist the Stamp Act.
September 28, 1768	British troops arrive in Boston.
March 5, 1770	Boston Massacre
November 28, 1773	Boston Tea Party
April 19, 1775	Battles of Lexington and Concord
June 17, 1775	Battle of Bunker Hill
March 17, 1776	British Evacuation Day

THE AMERICAN REVOLUTION

The conflict with England, called the American Revolution or the War of Independence, was entirely over colonialism, which was the geopolitical system in place at the time. The seeds of that conflict were planted when the Pilgrims and the Puritans left England. The colonists were in

North America to build a new and prosperous life as economic opportunity was very limited or absent in England. There was an implied contract that emphasized mutual benefit between the mother country and the colonies. Although England and Scotland had united in 1707, it should be kept in mind that England was the preeminent power in that union. The seat of government was in England and the Monarch, George III was English, the third monarch of the Hanover lineage. In addition, most of the trade was between England and the New World. When the English, or the British, started to limit opportunity in the colonies, they violated the spirit of the contract. The revolution was brought about by the economic abuses of colonialism—economic manipulations by England. That included ill-advised taxes and tariffs and other economic legislation that favored trade with England and limited the opportunities of the colonies for their own economic development. They passed oppressive legislation without giving much thought to possible repercussions and then backed off from it many times when they saw the negative reactions. But in doing so, they increased the hostility of the colonists with legislative provocation heaped upon provocation. Ultimately, that legislation led to the American Revolution. The revolution was not a retreat from our English heritage, which was never under dispute.

Garrisoning troops in the colonies, a very shortsighted strategy by the British, was an incitement to war. It inevitably would lead to conflict as occurred in the Boston Massacre. However, there were other incitements such as the Stamp Act that provoked active resistance. By this I mean that the local colonial government rejected the measure and recommended noncompliance. Along those lines, in addition to Massachusetts, there was active resistance in New York, Rhode Island, Maryland, Virginia, Georgia, and North Carolina.

Although it was an armed conflict between two parties, it was not an armed conflict between enemies. There was armed resistance to colonial rule and the British sent an expeditionary force to quell the rebellion. It was that initially but after a period of time, it became a war with the colonial forces pitted against the British forces. For the colonies, it was a war of independence, and it was a revolution, but for the British it was a civil war. The British considered the people in the colonies no different from the people in Britain—they were all British subjects. The people in the colonies had grown up there, but there was a heavy English influence on them—language, literature, religious orientation in many instances, culture, and heritage—all the same.

Each side had strengths and weaknesses. The British advantage was warfare at sea. In warfare on land, they were accustomed to conventional combat. But in unconventional warfare, they had a disadvantage. On land they fought in formation, a method that went back to antiquity, much like the Romans did in their time. With that method, they were best in open and flat terrain and were weaker in hills and mountains and in other unconventional battlegrounds. For example, on Lexington Common, the British had an advantage. In Concord, they also had an advantage. They were weaker in unfamiliar territory. They had difficulties in battles with irregulars. Because of the long distance between England and the colonies, they had provisioning problems as well.

A major strength of the colonies was the militia that was maintained by each colony. They also had a large population advantage and potentially the army could easily outnumber the British troops. The colonists were strong in the local territories because they knew them well. Roads, hills, valleys, towns, routes—they had a very good knowledge of all of that.

The British interests centered on trade and taxes. Before the fifteen years that preceded the revolution, the local governments in the colonies functioned autonomously in many respects and took care of most matters without any interference from England. Consequently, the colonies had strong governments in place that could take action when the revolution erupted. The British underestimated the strength of those governments when they tipped to the side of independence. Blame cannot be solely placed on the monarchy in England—it was England's entire geopolitical system that was the problem. It obviously did not understand the dangerous consequences of their incitements. It did not understand how powerful the forces of revolution could be.

DESTINY FAVORED INDEPENDENCE FOR THE COLONIES

The fundamental reason for independence was the fact that the colonists had a very different identity than the British. It was an identity that developed in the first generation of settlers in the New World. Among the colonists there was an independent spirit and ingenuity that propelled them forward and the will and resources to prevail. They could interrupt trade with Britain, which was dependent on the colonies for trade. They had experience with local affairs and the infrastructure and administration to govern independently. They also had militias that could aid in the revolution and that would form the basis of the Continental army.

On the side of Britain there were multiple factors that weakened their position and favored independence as well. First, the British interest was narrowly focused on trade, taxes, and tariffs. Second, there was lack of resolve among the British to enforce all of the provisions of the laws they put into place. There was considerable support for the positions of the colonists on many issues in England. The mother country had difficulty governing without the consent of the colonists, particularly when the governing concerned a narrow range of economic interests favoring England. The taxes and tariffs were so widely disregarded that the task of enforcement was impossible.

Britain was not prepared for a civil war. There was no enemy in the colonies, and that further weakened their resolve, favoring independence as an outcome. And in planning to use force, they underestimated the size of the force it would take to rule the colonies, considering the large area involved. For example, in Massachusetts, they had a token force, and it was only in the town of Boston. England was small compared with the thirteen colonies, whose land expanse was large and unfamiliar, being very different from anything they encountered in the Old World. It had great difficulty maintaining an army in the colonies because of provisioning limitations.

COMMENTS ON THE PRESENTATION OF HISTORY

The American Revolution has immense historical importance for our country. We must always present the events and implications of history as accurately as possible, even if the history is unfavorable to one side or another. Otherwise, we never learn anything from it. We must never attempt to revise history or hold back in its presentation because circumstances have changed between the countries involved. Trying to sweep unpleasant details under the rug is not ideal. We must never hesitate to engage in discourse about history. Being able to discuss the history of the American Revolution strengthens our bond with the United Kingdom, our closest ally, with which we share a common heritage. That bond survived the revolution and remains strong to this day. It was not England that was our enemy; it was its abuses of colonial rule. We should celebrate our Independence from the British Empire, but we must also celebrate our English heritage, an integral part of the fabric of our democratic society.

IN 1876, THE CENTENNIAL YEAR OF THE INDEPENDENCE OF THE UNITED STATES OF AMERICA

In the summer of the year 1876 on the hundredth anniversary or centennial of our independence, logic would suggest that there should have been an atmosphere of pride and exhilaration. There had been many national accomplishments over the first hundred years. The population had grown from four million in 1790 to thirty-two million in 1860, and by 1876 the number of states had grown to thirty-eight. The westward expansion of the country was in full force. That pattern of geographical growth was called "manifest destiny," because with a growing population, the nation's development required accessing the natural resources and land west of the Mississippi, and that began with the Louisiana Purchase, which doubled the size of the country. However, the spirit of the country was lowered by the Civil War and the Reconstruction period that followed it. Perhaps that was the reason that celebrations of the centennial were few and muted.

On Independence Day of 1876, Boston and the rest of the country were preoccupied with the Great American Pastime, baseball. The National Association of Baseball Players had folded after the close of the 1875 season. In its place came the National League of Professional Baseball Clubs. In 1876, New York was 251 years old, Boston was 246 years old, Philadelphia was 194 years old, and Chicago was only 43 years old. But in the new National League, all the teams were less than one-year-old. In the first game of the season, the Boston Red Caps defeated the Philadelphia Athletics by a score of 6–5. The Chicago White Stockings finished the season at the head of the pack with 52 wins and 14 losses. The memory of Joe Borden's no-hitter for the Boston Red Stockings on July 28, 1875, was fresh in mind when George Bradley pitched the first no-hitter in the new league for the Saint Louis Brown Stockings on July 15, 1876. There is no event in baseball as dramatic and exciting as a no-hitter. The thrill begins after two innings with no hits. Then with each new inning, the excitement builds, as does the trepidation over a ball possibly getting past the infield as a hit. I experienced that firsthand at age twelve sitting alone in the third base stands in Ebbets Field when Carl Erskine of the Brooklyn Dodgers blanked the Chicago Cubs 5–0 on June 19, 1952.

ALAN BALSAM

A GIFT FROM THE MOTHERS OF 1876 TO THE DAUGHTERS OF 1976

It would be difficult for a mother of 1876 to envision a daughter of 1976, but there is no question that the achievements of the early activists in the women's rights movement are a great legacy for women of future generations. On July 4, 1876, there was a celebration of the centennial in Philadelphia. Women's rights activists, having not been invited to participate in the program of the celebration of the birth of the nation, petitioned the chair of the event, General Joseph Hawley, for the opportunity to present their own Declaration of Independence. Mrs. Sara Andrews Spencer presented a letter from Mrs. Elizabeth Stanton, president of the association, requesting permission to make a simple presentation at the end of the program. When that request was denied because the program had already been prepared, the suffragettes staged a type of sit-in.

At an opportune time during the program, lack of authorization notwithstanding, Miss Susan B. Anthony rose to her feet and began to read the Declaration of Rights for Women by the National Woman Suffrage Association, July 4, 1786, to a sympathetic and receptive audience. It's true they were out of order. The general had said that they were there to celebrate what had been done in the last one hundred years, not what had not been done. But a gavel in the hand of a general is no match for women with a righteous cause, and Ms. Anthony read the declaration from beginning to end. That document underscored the fact that women did not have the full rights of citizenship as they were not allowed to vote. Noted was that habeas corpus rights were improperly suspended in the case of a married woman against her husband in all states of the union. The right to trial by a jury of peers for women was not possible either, as women did not serve on juries. Numerous other inequalities in the treatment of women were cited as well. It also followed the general pattern that lack of enfranchisement gives rise to pervasive infringements on the civil rights of those affected. And as a reminder that achieving human rights involves many groups and is an ongoing battle, it should be noted that at the centennial celebration, there was no representation for the children of our country. They desperately needed a bill of rights before, during and after that era, but such a document is lacking to this very day!

A VISIT TO DOWNTOWN BOSTON IN THE BICENTENNIAL PERIOD

I was heading downtown on the T, and my destination was Park Street station. The population of Downtown swells during the day and recedes in the evening. Each of the Green Line branches leads to Park Street station, which was the first station to be built on the T. All the commuters on the Green Line come from the west, from various neighborhoods in Newton and Brookline. The cars tend to fill early in their route during rush hour so a seat is never guaranteed, but I was happy to stand and hold onto a pole or the swinging handles above the seats. I felt the ride more while standing being, jostled about at the turns and with changes in speed but I could often see much more.

That day the car was filled with younger people dressed for business, and I detected bright looks on their faces, and to me that was a sign of great hope. I observed that there was very little interaction among the commuters. The seats face in various directions, and I often saw people reading paperbacks and sometimes businesspersons working on proposals. The train emptied, to a large extent, at Park Street, the only Green Line station in Downtown. And after the doors opened, I was swept out with the tide of commuters whose destination was Downtown.

A BLIND WOMAN WALKING IN THE STREETS OF BOSTON

I walked up the stairs and exited the station at Park Street and made my way to a point nearby—the north corner of Tremont and Winter Streets—and there I heard a tapping sound that I recognized. It was coming from the white cane of a blind woman that was striking the very lowest portion of the buildings as she passed them. When she came to an entrance to a building, she would slow her pace. She was using the cane to locate landmarks on the street. She proceeded without difficulty. I noted that she listened carefully to the sound of each tap as the tip of the cane struck concrete of the buildings. She was walking up Tremont Street. She had no trouble walking along the street, and when she came to the corner she listened for traffic. Someone offered to help her cross the street. She accepted and then was on her own.

I had seen her many times before. Occasionally she would cross the street on her own, with the cane held in front of her, tapping on the asphalt in a side-to-side radius. I was always thrilled to see how well she was able to maneuver with her head held erect and looking straight ahead. Her route was the same each time I observed her. On several occasions, I noted her coming out of the T station. She was able to climb the stairs once she found the banister on one side. She could handle the landings without difficulty, and before long she was out on the sidewalk moving to her destination. I always found her to be the personification of courage and a true inspiration—it was difficult to fathom how she developed the special skills required to move about in the environment in the absence of vision. I could sense from the way she moved about with the cane that she had been blind for many years, perhaps even from birth. Moreover, it was very clear that she had a lot of experience using the cane. Because the tapping had a distinct pitch when various objects were struck, she seemed to know exactly where she was by the tapping. She never lifted the cane more than a few inches from the ground. She inspired me in a way that whenever I thought something was impossible to do, I thought of her. I can think of no more inhospitable environment for a blind person than the T and the city streets, and what I would have thought to be impossible, she showed was indeed possible.

Many blind children were educated at the Perkins School for the Blind in Watertown, Massachusetts, established in 1829. Their mission to this day has been "to prepare children who are blind with the education, tools, and skills they need to realize their potential."

Not far from the intersection of Winter and Washington Streets is a building that housed the laboratory of Dr. Alexander Graham Bell. The corner building at Avenue de Lafayette and Harrison Avenue Extension was where the telephone was first used by Dr. Bell to summon his associate, Dr. Watson from another room. Not far from there was a building on Chauncy Street at the edge of Chinatown, where I served as a medical consultant to the Disability Determination Services. The building was constructed in the art deco style with a spacious and nicely appointed lobby. There are many buildings with that style in the downtown area.

DOWNTOWN CROSSING

I walked from Chauncy Street to Downtown Crossing. At that time in that area there was a general pattern of pedestrian traffic. Winter Street brought you directly to Downtown Crossing about a block away. You could also gain access to Winter Street via Hamilton Place. Viewing Hamilton Place from Tremont gave the impression that it was a blind alley that ended at the Orpheum, but the street was actually shaped like an L with the longer limb of the street emptying onto Winter Street. Winter Street near Tremont had seen better days. It was the site of the old Boston Music Hall and the home of the Boston Symphony for almost half a century. However, in the late 1800s there was much public transportation construction below and above ground that interfered with access to the area. The Boston Symphony moved out to a new concert hall, Symphony Hall, in Back Bay. Well before that many of the churches in Downtown had moved out to Back Bay, as the church elders were seeking a more savory environment. The departure of the music hall signaled the beginning of the area's decline. The old Boston Music Hall yielded to the Orpheum and vaudeville, and the character of the area started its downhill spiral to populism setting the scene for Downtown Crossing of the modern era.

Winter Street between Tremont and Washington Street was open to vehicular traffic, but as it continued beyond that intersection, it was closed to traffic for at least a block with a pedestrian mall called Downtown Crossing at the location. The pedestrian traffic on the mall was never orderly. People would walk in just about any direction. The area had department stores and a few small shops and a bank. It was the site of outdoor performances, small political demonstrations, and sidewalk beggars, and there was always hustle and bustle in the area as the pedestrian traffic from various streets emptied into the mall. It seemed like the land of Everyman, an extension of the Boston Common from the west and of city hall from the north. In the summer it was busier than in the winter because of the favorable weather. It was a unique place in the sense that people were the center of attention there. They were milling about and gathering in small groups to observe a performance or demonstration.

The area has many nondescript features, but it is not without charm. At the time, there was a beggar who sat motionless on the ground with his open cap in front of him. I had seen him on several occasions, and he would be staring downward, not paying any attention to people walking by. He appeared to have an expressionless face. He was tall—you could get a sense of his height from how he appeared sitting—and thin. The pedestrians seemed to pay little attention to him—I got the sense that most were avoiding him. I was curious about his background. He was not unkempt in any way, and he certainly appeared able-bodied. He was an enigma.

I was thinking of trying to engage him in some conversation, but I hesitated to do so as he seemed to be in a trance or meditating, and I felt that any gesture on my part would be unheeded. The man sat with his back resting against the base of Filene's department store window. He sat in an area that was not far from Saint Anthony's Shrine less than a block away. I had seen him many times that way, and the scene upon repetition gained emphasis and urgency in my mind; I resolved to try to talk to him. I thought, *Perhaps he is depressed; perhaps there is some help or direction I could give him.*

The next time I saw the man I was relieved as the situation had changed. He was standing on his feet engaged in an animated conversation with another man. He was smiling, and his appearance had changed completely. I understood that I was viewing the actual person at that time while before I was seeing someone else.

The Downtown Crossing area was a mixed area. There were some small stores that were unoccupied and in disrepair. I had read an interesting article in the newspaper about the reclamation of one of those sites by a businessman. The man had bought one of the properties with the idea of creating a tavern in it. The design was rather elaborate as there were two floors. The renovation was accomplished, and the pub had an official opening. I was familiar with the property, and I knew what it looked like before the renovations were done and had the opportunity to see it afterward. It was attractive but very small. Then I came to a paragraph in the article that mentioned the amount of money the proprietor had spent on the project: $5 million—that amount made no sense as the space was too small—I would say $500,000 would cover those renovations. I felt that there was intent to describe the venture with hyperbole, but I couldn't figure out why. It was as if the proprietor had a few drinks too many before giving the reporter the information. Interestingly, it appeared that the reporter accepted the owner's version of the cost of the project rather uncritically.

SCHOOL STREET: A CITY BLOCK THAT WAS AN EARLY BOSTON NEIGHBORHOOD

The intersection of School Street and Tremont Street is a gateway to Downtown with School Street bringing you to that area. The School Street square block shown in a plat from 1648 below has a long and venerable history in Boston. It is the extension of Beacon Street so it is a direct walking route for people from Beacon Hill. The School Street square block bordered by Tremont to the west, Washington Street to the east, and Court Street to the north was one of the earliest areas in Boston and is clearly outlined in a map from the mid-1600s. In the early history of the town of Boston, it had a burying ground at the corner of Tremont, a school at the center of the block and a jail on Court Street—in the area opposite the school. At the southwest corner stands Kings Chapel and the old burying ground. As you walk down School Street, which is a very narrow street, toward Washington Street, on the right you pass a hotel and several office buildings in the art deco style, and on the left you come upon old city hall, which is a rather ornate structure built in the French Second Empire style with a statue of Benjamin Franklin on its right. The old city hall stands in the lot where the school was located in the 1600s and, after that, at 45 School Street. The building was constructed between 1862 and 1865. It was the center of city government until 1969 when the new city hall came into use. The building, being on the smaller scale, at times could be very crowded with people, mostly lobbyists, especially in the early 1900s. The School Street block was a popular location for doctors and pharmacists. Dr. John Warren, the younger brother of the patriot, Dr. Joseph Warren, resided at 27 School Street and had his medical office there. Farther down the block on the old city hall side, at the corner of Washington Street, stands the Corner Bookstore, one of the earliest brick buildings in Boston.

The old city hall building has a courtyard, and at its right side, facing the street, stands a statue of Benjamin Franklin, who was born in 1706 in a house on nearby Milk Street to a Puritan family, one of seventeen children. He was mostly self-educated, as he left school at age ten. He was a beloved elder statesman at the time of the American Revolution, and he had important diplomatic roles in Europe as an advocate for independence for the North American colonies. His early career started in the family's printing business and, at age seventeen, he left Massachusetts for Pennsylvania in search of opportunity. He started a publishing business of his own and was very successful with that. Outside the realm of publishing and public service, he had many talents and made significant contributions in science to the understanding that lightning was a form of electricity. Although he lacked formal education, he was a patron of education, in addition to being an inventor, so it is both ironic and appropriate that the statue of Franklin is facing School Street.

At the time the Corner Bookstore was built, Washington Street was called High Street. In earlier years it was the site of the house of Anne Hutchinson, expelled from the town in 1638 because of heresy. Her house fell victim to a fire and was destroyed in the early 1700s, and the lot was bought by Thomas Crease, the apothecary, to build his residence and shop. In later years, beginning when first-floor space of the Crease building was used for various commercial purposes, there were various alterations made to the structure, particularly involving the first floor, which fronts on the two streets. Its name derives from its use as a bookstore. It also served as a meeting place for American authors, including Longfellow, Emerson, Hawthorne, and Holmes, each born just after the turn of the century of the revolution, during the first ten years of the nineteenth century. Those authors were raised in the aftermath of the American Revolution when the history of the events was mostly oral, related by their parents, who experienced it when they were children. They traded stories about local history, including those related to the American Revolution, and one of those stories is recounted by Longfellow in "The Midnight Ride of Paul Revere." The corner position of the building is an important feature, which over a long period of time has appealed to various small businesses. One important practical lesson we can learn from this building is that commercial enterprises may come and go, but a good location, particularly a corner site, always remains in demand.

The building is in the Georgian style and features ground-floor display windows and entrances. The windows have a lattice pattern with multiple windowpanes in double-hung sashes. Window size becomes smaller at higher levels, and the gambrel roof has two gables, with dormer windows and triangular pediment roofs. The building displays only two sides, the larger of which fronts on School Street and the smaller on Washington Street. On the School Street side, moving upward above the first level, the number of windows decreases as the building width tapers, and the window pattern is five, three, and one. And because space in the downtown area is at such a premium, especially at a good location, we only see two sides of the Corner Book Store. The original plats for the lots and the houses built on them showed plenty of yard space, but as time moved, on the buildings were constructed side by side with no intervening space.

The old state house is located very close to the School Street square block. The Court Street side of the square block spills into State Street, formerly King Street in the colonial era. The old state house is situated diagonally across the way from the western corner of Court Street. The earliest building dating back to 1657 was a wooden structure. It fell victim to a fire and was replaced in 1712. On the first floor it had a merchants' exchange, and there was a warehouse in the basement. It housed various governmental bodies including the council chamber of the royal governor and chambers for various courts. The building has seen many changes and upgrades over the years. It became the Massachusetts state house from 1776 to 1778 and Boston's city hall from 1830 to 1841. In 1881 it became a museum and remains so as of the present time.

The old state house was built in the Georgian style and has a great location; it appears to be situated on an island-like city block. The two-story building has a wonderful three-dimensional balanced presentation, and it appears as a central element framed by nearby tall buildings. It is a two-story brick building with a gabled roof and a rectangular double-tower projection from the roof's center. The tower pedestal holds a white two-story tower, with each story having an ornamental low partition, and there are generously proportioned tablet-shaped windows on each of the sides of the two tower elements. The upper portion is topped by a finial with a decorative weather vane. The aesthetic elements on the end facades of the building display ornate decorations that date back to the colonial era. The lion and the unicorn are symbols of the English monarch and the clock in between them symbolizes the transience of imperial power in our nation's history. On the second-floor end facade there is a balcony at the base of a decorative framed central windowed entryway.

THE REBUILDING OF DOWNTOWN BOSTON

Anytime a new building was constructed in downtown Boston was a time for celebration. The area was so frozen in history and modernization was so desperately needed that the redevelopment of the area was welcome, a step in the right direction. Each new building offered the promise of modernization bringing relief from the unchanging historical landscape and the heavy hand of architectural preservationism felt everywhere in the area.

THE NEW AND THE OLD, SIDE BY SIDE: THE NEXUS OF BUSINESS, ARCHITECTURE, AND HISTORY

In most instances, the architecture of the new office buildings Downtown is original, and the degree of innovation visible in some of the designs is truly inspiring. Each new building reflects very important human dimensions—creativity in architecture and development in business—that offer hope for the future. We must understand that preserving the past is not a deterrent to developing the future. Development brings vitality; preserving the past does not. Preservation is important, but it looks backward, and what one must do is look forward. This is a very important general principle. The whole society needs to move forward, and you can't do it unless you create new things. Business, in order to be competitive, has to develop. This is why the most important feature of Downtown is the new, as it offers hope for the future. New ideas and new businesses are very much needed. People tend to reject anything different—unaccepting and discouraging of new things—however, there is only transient hope in the status quo, and over time that approach leads to stagnation. It's a problem. The terms that I use to describe the new construction of skyscrapers in downtown Boston are rebirth, rejuvenation, and modernization. And we see architecture and history intertwined. History is preserved, but development is not curtailed. We see that the downtown area has had enlightened development. The old and the new stand side by side. There was no attempt to hold back the new—it was encouraged and the new, besides having its own functionality, is plainly seen to be in reasonable balance with the old.

PRIVATE SECTOR INITIATIVES

It is correct to say there is a partnership between the public and private sectors. The public sector's role is often highly overrated. Most of the real effort comes from the private sector. The public sector is so often simply a review and an approval. Whenever you suddenly see a large amount of commercial building in one area there are often some important factors that were holding back development in that area hitherto. There are several possibilities. First, politics may be a factor. Parochialism in local governance tends to inhibit outside capital investment. Parochialism tends to thrive where the electorate overemphasizes popularity versus substance, such as in long or unlimited terms of service. In general, life terms in a given office tend to encourage parochialism, the status quo, and lack of outside investment, discouraging innovation. Then the physical area is very small, and that could limit opportunity as well.

Then there is historical context. The old guard, the Brahmins, had waning power, and their rule was largely based on the accomplishments of earlier generations. The old guard tended to be stodgy and antibusiness in the sense that it preferred passive fiduciary roles rather than active roles. The new guard, the immigrants, did not have a proper model in the old guard, and the new guard was very involved in social welfare issues.

Also, there is the conflicting interest of historical preservationism. Preserving older structures slows the development of newer structures. Also, most of the more heavily populated neighborhoods in Boston were constituents for themselves, but the downtown area, with its limited population, did not have a significant voting constituency. It would be difficult to know which of these factors had the greatest effect on limiting development. At any rate, whatever signaled the change that brought about the building spurt Downtown was welcome. That renewal depended on outside capital investment. Only a limited number of banks and insurance companies required new buildings. But once outside capital came to the area, it experienced dramatic growth. The commercial real estate boom in the downtown area was indeed a sign of renewal. The economy in Massachusetts—heavily centered on technology, education, and medicine—requires more diversification. This will occur when entrepreneurial spirit is given as much emphasis as is the institutional spirit.

THE BUSINESS LANDSCAPE: DOWNTOWN SKYSCRAPERS

In the bicentennial era, there was optimism that gave rise to hope and rebuilding. The hallmark building of most downtown areas is the skyscraper. The development of very tall buildings in Boston moved at a very slow pace until the decade of the bicentennial. During that period there was tremendous growth in the construction of skyscrapers Downtown. The earliest tall building in Boston, but not quite a skyscraper, was the thirteen-story Ames Building constructed in 1893. The Custom House Tower, built in the art deco style in 1915 and a genuine skyscraper at a height of 496 feet, is architecturally one of the finest modern buildings ever built in Boston. The State Street Bank building was erected in 1966. There was a major building boom in the downtown area starting in the decade of the bicentennial. Harbor Towers, a residential high-rise, was built in 1970. The earliest commercial building was the Bank of Boston at 100 Federal Street—it was completed in 1971 and reached a height of 591 feet. The tallest building in the area at about that time was the Federal Reserve Bank tower, which is 614 feet high, built in 1972–1974. Those two skyscrapers were the only ones that were completed before the bicentennial on July 4, 1976. Following their construction, there were several new additions to the downtown area from the middle 1970s to the early 1990s.

FEDERAL RESERVE BANK BUILDING

The Federal Reserve Bank Building and Plaza was completed in 1974. With capital, some long-term investment thinking, and a good architectural team, there was the rare opportunity to create "something out of nothing." A typical warehouse site on a wharf, in a peripheral location, was transformed by a federal bank. A government building that reflects the imagination and creativity of the private sector, it looks as unique and interesting today as it did when it was first built. The only skyscraper built on a wharf, it looks out at Boston Harbor and is very close to the Tea Party wharf.

THE FINANCIAL DISTRICT

The financial district of Boston is composed of banks, investment companies, insurance companies, and other business establishments. The area has witnessed the growth of the financial industry, and much of the modern architecture can be found in that district. The newer buildings were built starting in the decade of the bicentennial. There were a few that were constructed before that, but most were built at that time or later.

There were many buildings that I would have been very happy to own. When I mention a building whose ownership has changed hands, I refer to it as the building of the original owners, who actually built the property. I wouldn't want to own a boxlike structure like the Bank of New England building, but I would be very happy to own Bank of Boston's building. I consider it a masterpiece of modern architecture.

The Bank of Boston building, completed in 1971, is one of the tallest buildings in Boston at 591 feet in height. It stands alone on a gore, and it displays very much the same pattern from each of its four sides. A wraparound boxlike lower element about eight stories high projects over the sidewalks, and its base angulates to an even narrower rectangular base, which has the appearance of a pedestal for the building. A rectangular tower rises up from the lower element. It is built of highly polished maroon granite that reflects light and the images of other buildings can be seen on the four sides of the building. The tower of the building can be identified from many different sites in the area.

There are many things I like about this building, all of which I believe contribute to its uniqueness. The building has wonderful 360 degree symmetry, and I like its geometric forms and balance. It has a very interesting ground level presentation, and it also has excellent visual appeal at a distance—it captures the attention immediately. I particularly like the highly polished granite facade and its pleasant tone. I also like its presentation in space on a gore. It is separated from all other buildings by city streets.

The First National Bank of Boston was established in 1784. It had over two hundred years of business experience, and what a great business outfit it was. The bank, commonly referred to as Bank of Boston, had class, character, and very good taste. I was privileged to have them as a tenant on the first floor in my building in Worcester. They were old fashioned in some ways, but they had very high integrity and such great potential. They valued quality, and the building they built in Downtown Boston reflected that approach. Their contributions were not appreciated adequately—but nonetheless, I think the decision to sell the bank to Fleet was incorrect. It causes me great anguish to come to grips with the fact that they sold out to another bank. It was a colossal mistake. It shows that any institution's survival can be jeopardized if it gets into the wrong hands. The loss of Bank of Boston, a venerable financial institution, was a disaster for Boston that will continue to be felt in years to come. If I could, I would buy back Bank of Boston from Bank of America and return it to 100 Federal Street where it belongs.

Often a bank, like any other business, makes many decisions that turn out to be justified and others that turn out to be ill advised, but the latter of which only becomes clear in retrospect. For example, banks are always looking to expand their businesses, and in the era of commercial development ushered in by the bicentennial that was particularly true. Bank of Boston was interested in expanding its business cities and towns west of Boston. At the time, they had a small office in downtown Worcester, in the building I owned at the corner of Main and Foster streets. They realized that in order to expand business in the Boston, Worcester, Providence triangle, they needed a stronger presence in Worcester, so they expanded at that location.

In Boston itself, however, one of their attempts at expansion seemed to make very little sense. At the time, in Boston there was a lot of emphasis on small multiple branches to provide easy access to pedestrian traffic. It seemed that every week a new bank branch would open. Following that trend, Bank of Boston decided to open a branch on Temple Place. The building itself was very impressive—it looked like a bank in so many respects, but the location made no sense. There was little on Temple Place to attract pedestrian traffic. The major entrance to Downtown was via Winter Street and Downtown Crossing. The reason that Winter Street was the main route was twofold: first, Park Street station let out nearby and second, pedestrian traffic from Boylston Street would tend to avoid continuing on Boylston Street to downtown because the area was too seedy, making it unwalkable. The place to be was Winter Street, but Bank of Boston was just a few blocks away on Federal Street; hence, there was no need for a branch in such close proximity to the bank's principal location.

POST OFFICE SQUARE

Post Office Square is a rectangular area in downtown Boston that contains the post office in one corner. The square is bordered by Congress Street on the west, Pearl Street on the east and Franklin Street on the south and Water Street on the north. The Boston post office is located at the corner of Congress and Water streets. The square features high-rise buildings on Congress and Pearl streets and a small park in the center of the square.

The square dates back to the early 1870s. In the eighteen hundreds, the area was mostly commercial, and there were office buildings around the square as there are today. Unfortunately, none of the original buildings survived. One of the original buildings, the old post office, was built in the Second Empire style. It was a very ornate and unusual building with arched and framed windows and gables in the roof. In addition, it had a pyramid-shaped central tower that rose above a central motif.

In the 1930s, the United States was in the grips of the Great Depression. In retrospect it seems so ironic that one of the streets in Post Office Square is named Franklin Street, after Benjamin Franklin, the American patriot and diplomat. When the new post office was built, however, a different Franklin was in office, Franklin Roosevelt. The first Franklin was a self-proclaimed penny pincher, but the second Franklin had the opposite tendency and the New Deal was a good example of that. In 1933, when the new post office was built, it was the second Franklin's approach that was needed in our country, and there were not many people who disagreed.

In that era, the old Boston post office was demolished, and a new one was constructed. Sadly, the old post office building, an architectural delight, was not preserved. Today, if a larger and new building is needed, a new site would be purchased for it to be built there. For example, when city hall moved to its new building, the old city hall was left intact and a new use was found for it. In place of the old post office a new one was built—a very tall building was constructed in the art deco style, and that became the new post office and court building.

The art deco pattern is without a doubt the most important and influential architectural style of the modern era, starting in the early 1900s. An outgrowth of the arts and crafts movement at the turn of the century, it had a pervasive influence that affected design, including the exterior and interior of public buildings, furniture, and luxury products. It is a bold style that uses generous proportions and favors symmetry and rectilinear presentation, color motifs, and ornamentation. The buildings often display recessed upper stories, a very common design feature. Also, the architecture favors buildings that are tall and thin. Decorative columns incorporated into the facade of the structure are tall, flat, and often fluted. The ornamentation is derived from various sources. The depiction of the human form is generally oversized and dramatic, and figures are often depicted in motion.

Artistically, art deco architecture is a product of various movements in art including cubism, constructivism, functionalism, modernism and futurism. The art deco architecture first appeared in Paris at about 1910 with the building of the Theatre des Champs-Elysees. The style soon became very popular in the United States, where it was taken to new heights starting in the late 1920s. The style became much more flamboyant, and at a time when there was much new construction in the cities of the United States, the art deco style flourished and captured the imagination. The style was considered luxurious and glamorous, and it dominated the modern architectural scene for many years. New York City's Radio City Music Hall, built in 1930, is an early example of the pattern. Some of the buildings in Boston built around the time of the bicentennial have exterior color motifs borrowed from the art deco era. Art deco architecture is clearly an important part of the charm of Downtown.

We can say that the new post office was a progeny of the art deco period. It has a tall structure with an imposing facade that affords it a strong frontal appearance. There are two rectangular towers that rise to either side of the entrance. The facade of the building has a flat rectilinear appearance typical of art deco structures. In the neighborhood of Post Office Square there is a very impressive art deco building at 75 Franklin Street at the corner of Federal. It has a strong presentation from all views. It has recessed floors at the upper levels. It is perhaps the best high-style example of an art deco building in the city besides the Custom House Tower, which is a distinguished example of early art deco style in the city. Another building in that style, the New England Telephone Building, which was built in 1947, rises in Post Office Square on Franklin Street.

In earlier days, as a consequence of weak zoning laws, an open outdoor parking garage, an eyesore, occupied the center of the square. That was rectified when the garage was relocated to underground and a park was built above it. The park, an inner city man-made nature sanctuary, has many interesting features including a nice selection of plants and trees. However, the views of the architecture of the buildings in the square is somewhat obscured by the trees in this pleasant niche park.

The buildings in Post Office Square, in addition to the post office and the telephone company building, include a miscellany of other office buildings and a hotel located in the old Federal Reserve Bank at the corner of Franklin and Pearl Streets.

The new Boston city hall, which displays a modernistic architectural style, has considerable artistic merit and should not be dismissed simply because it is different. The pattern is very unique and captures attention. The style has been called "brutalism" but I disagree with that appellation as it has a negative connotation; I would prefer to call it "avant garde." The building has many interesting features. It is stark with bold geometric designs that feature frontalism as there is an emphasis on width as opposed to height. Hence, it is difficult to find a vantage point that presents a three-dimensional view of the structure. However, there are many buildings in Boston for which this is also true.

Nevertheless, the architecture is bold, with many interesting features, and no building in that area can compete with its originality. I find the tapering of the floors in an inverted pattern interesting, as well as the lower facade. The narrow vertical windows have a grid-like appearance. However, there is too much emphasis on concrete, which gives it a prefabricated look. Government Center shows too much concrete as opposed to lawns; although they would require considerable maintenance, they have much more charm and interest. And there is much that can be done to update the area, which needs it. In addition, the location tends to be less favorable than most of Downtown as it edges back against the freeway. The frequent presence of parked vehicles next to the building is an aesthetic detraction. But overall, there is much that can be done to enhance the appearance and charm of the building.

The space in front of new city hall also needs upgrading. It has a vacant and sterile appearance, which exaggerates the starkness of the building. The sea of concrete at the foot of the building does not enhance its image. It is a detraction to have such a large vacant space in front of the building.

A visit to Downtown in the summer of the bicentennial era has revealed a mixture of buildings, some old and some new. The influence of earlier history is felt with every step walking through the area. The summer season, a perfect time for a visit to the area, has a less hectic pace of activity. Emptied of people who have temporarily relocated to the seashore or the mountains, either on vacation or on day trips, Downtown has fewer distractions than when it is dense with people. As summer yields to autumn, however, they will return. Next, we move to a different area in Boston and turn our attention to the sights of autumn.

AUTUMN IN BACK BAY AND THE PUBLIC GARDEN

AUTUMN IN NEW ENGLAND

Autumn in New England is a season of changes—some come on abruptly and others gradually. The transition period from summer to autumn can be quite variable. Occasionally, summer seems to linger, and there is hardly any interruption in the warm weather. The saying that you can't judge the calendar by the weather holds true just as much as the reverse. In a momentary lapse in memory, you could identify a particular day as being in summer when it is actually in autumn. This pattern is called Indian summer, and the temperatures remain warm in September and early October. Indian summer was likely much appreciated by the American Indians, as it provided additional time with favorable hunting conditions before the geese and ducks left in the fall. In Indian summer, autumn creeps along on cat feet, mostly unnoticed.

The usual signs of autumn appear late in the season and seem to come on rather suddenly. Then comes one day in which an unusually cool breeze heralds the appearance of fall. In autumn in Boston, with no Indian summer, the weather is noticeably cooler; the average daily temperature in October ranges from a high of 62 degrees to a low of 46 degrees.

In autumn, the music of summer ends as the songbirds fly southward. The baseball season ends, and in Boston, as well as most other cities with teams in the league, winning the pennant remains elusive for yet another year. Not to worry, there is always a chance that things will be different next year. Generally, the angst over losing this year's pennant is very short-lived, giving way to hopes of better fortune starting next spring. With loyal fans there is always hope for the future. The seeds of hope for the coming year are reflected in the emphatic but wistful and often unrealistic expression "Wait till next year!" In autumn, it is back to school and back to work after the recreational pursuits of summer, with shorter days as the clock is moved backward and darkness arrives earlier in the day.

As to plans and resolutions for the New Year, most of those occur in the summer rather than December, as the summer provides more opportunity for planning and the work effort often begins in autumn. The calendar year, however, runs from January to December, the fiscal year from July to June and there is no official year from September through August. In dress wear, long-sleeve shirts replace short-sleeve shirts; in recreation wear, the sweat shirt replaces the T-shirt; and sweaters and jackets reappear after the summer hiatus. Last, in autumn, the appearance of the trees changes as treetops take on splashes of color rivaling those of the artist's palette as their leaves inexorably change colors, heralding their imminent fall to the ground.

AUTUMN IS THE SEASON OF THE TREES

Autumn in New England is a poignant love affair between people and trees that occurs annually, beginning gradually as summer fades and ending abruptly when the trees become bare, signaling the approach of winter. The love itself, however, is unending and remains dormant in the unseen buds that will sprout and open the next spring. In the other seasons, trees ordinarily attract little attention; they are often silent elements, part of the background in the environment. Their leafy canopies are a sea of green that is part of the lush New England natural habitat. From a distance it is difficult to distinguish one tree from another. From that perspective, a stand of trees or an entire forest lacks individuality; it is the shape and coloration of the group that we recognize. But in autumn all that changes as the leaves change color. Then trees become the focus of our attention and they exert a powerful magnetism that draws people close to them. For many people, being in the presence of the great beauty of nature can be an awe-inspiring experience.

The treetops have cycles of renewal, as the leaves of the hardwood trees last about three-quarters of the year. Color change in the leaves signals their last period of life on the tree. There is no question that they leave the tree with a magnificent flourish of color. Early on while still attached to the branches, the leaves change their colors gradually from green to red to yellow, and then they fall from the trees. The various shades of red seem to attract the most attention since that color is so strong and dramatic. The leaf cycle of trees reflects changes in weather patterns in a given area. The leaves will not change their color until there is a noticeable change in the temperature and summer rains have come and gone. The change in color of leaves in a stand of trees is not necessarily synchronized—one tree is often more advanced than others.

In New England the change in the leaves starts in the north in the mountains and gradually moves southward. That is where the change begins as the cooler weather starts in more northerly high places. Gradually, the change in color of the trees moves southward, enveloping the entire Northeast including mountains and lowlands and coastal and inland areas. It is as if the colors from the north are borne on the wind and fall on the trees like rain from a cloud, spreading the pattern over the entire region. The visual impact is greatest when multiple trees are involved in the display, so the forest-covered mountains tend to attract the most attention. Deciduous trees are also prevalent in the cities and towns; whether in the backyard or on the city streets or in the parks, their change in color is fascinating to watch. The fallen leaves have unique interest as well. You can touch a fallen leaf and hold it up in the light to study its color pattern and shape. And fallen leaves are raised once again by the winds of autumn that carry them near and far. The flight of fallen leaves can be spectacular, for as the winds gather strength they often move the leaves in waves to various destinations. As autumn in Newton teaches us, anyone who takes on the task of clearing the leaves in the fall has the wonderful opportunity of handling them dry or wet and getting the feel of a deciduous tree's leaf, which is a magnificent creation of nature. You can turn it over in your hands and look at each side from multiple vantage points.

For interesting tree color, you don't have to go too far. You could leave the city and head for the country—Walden Pond in the hills of Concord would be a good choice for that purpose—the higher elevation and inland location intensify the color changes and the atmosphere in the hills is serene.

It was early in October on the weekend, and I had planned to devote most of the day to touring in Back Bay and the Public Garden. The weather was seasonal, so I wore a sweater for the trip, which began at the Chestnut Hill T station. I would estimate that it was about 50 degrees and a very clear autumn day, excellent for walking, and I chose a time that was favorable for viewing the trees. Sometimes, in Boston itself there comes a year that brings colorations to the leaves of autumn only transiently, and the changes are so rapid that they seem minimal as well. The weather in the season has a major influence. A wet September is unfavorable to the change in leaves, but a dry and cool September is favorable. The leaves had already started to fall from the trees—I knew that firsthand as I had collected them in the front and side yards at home in Oak Hill in Newton.

A TRIP TO BACK BAY AND THE PUBLIC GARDEN IN AUTUMN BEGINS ON HAMMOND STREET IN NEWTON

Hammond Street in the Chestnut Hill neighborhood is the gateway from the old to the new in the city of Newton. It is a route with much historical charm, and in Hammond Street you can feel Newton's kinship to Cambridge. Newton was first settled in 1630—initially it was called Newe Towne—and in 1638 it became part of Cambridge. The settlement of the area developed rapidly after the West Newton Indian tribe in Nonantum, a branch of the Massachusett Indians, relocated to Natick. Waban, its tribal leader, or sachem, became convinced that moving to the adjacent area was the best option at the time. Fifty years later, Newton separated from Cambridge to become an independent settlement, and in 1691 it took on its original name, Newtowne, which later evolved into Newton. It would probably be a reasonable hypothesis that the original European inhabitants of Hammond Street were mercantilists who wanted good access to Boston with two possible routes, Beacon Street and Boylston Street. Beacon Street, although primarily residential in character, is a very wide street; it is what most people would call an avenue. Of the two routes, Beacon Street provides a much more direct route to Boston through Brookline. While Boylston Street has mixed character—some residential but mostly small commercial buildings that are often offices in converted houses—it, too, is a major thoroughfare with avenue-sized proportions, though it takes a more tortuous route to Boston. Hammond Street winds its way from the center of Newton southward to the periphery, from Beacon Street to Boylston

Street. It is quite narrow and country-like, and the road itself is largely eclipsed by the mansions and their grounds on either side of the street. A highlight of the area is opulence of natural space on either side of street, unrivaled in most other residential enclaves in the area.

Starting at Boylston Street, the route to the T station along Hammond Street is lined with sizable oaks and maples and some little leaf lindens. The oaks and the maples look like they are more than one hundred years old. Considerably younger are members of the linden family of trees which are such a popular choice for street trees in the Northeast that I call the littleleaf linden, *Tilia cordata*, one of my favorite trees, Aunt Tillie. Chestnut trees are found in abundance in the area as well, and the neighborhood derives its name from those trees and the hill on which they were first planted. That route brings you past the Longwood Cricket Club and, as the road bears to the left, you cross a bridge over the T tracks and make a sharp right into the station parking lot. Just a moment before making that turn, judging from the surroundings, you would have no idea that there was or could be a train station hidden in the area. The T station grounds border the grounds of the Chestnut Hill School to the north, separated by a stone partition and those of the Brimmer and May School on the east. The latter's school grounds can only be seen with great effort as they are close to the T tracks heading westward. You have to stand on a bench or climb on to a low stone partition to catch a glimpse of the property. The entire area is surrounded by hardwood trees planted on neighboring properties and also at the perimeter of the station grounds. The leaves on the broadleaf trees were turning orange, and there were some leaves that had fallen to the ground and were being tossed about by wind and the also by gusts generated by passing cars.

I planned to travel to Back Bay indirectly that day, taking the D train on the Riverside Line to Longwood station, and from there to walk along Longwood Avenue heading in a southeasterly path toward Huntington Avenue, where I would take the E train to Copley Square; from there I would tour on foot. With the Massachusetts Bay Transportation Authority (MBTA) lines, like the major roads in Newton and Brookline, all routes lead to Boston. The Green Line branches in Newton and Brookline, like the branches of a tree once they emerge from its trunk have no connections one to another. The B, C, and D branches do, however, meet in Boston at Kenmore Square and the E line, which originates in Jamaica Plain, has no connection until it meets the other lines at Copley Square Station in Back Bay. However, my plan for the morning, as outlined above, would provide a walking connection between the D and E lines along Longwood Avenue.

I had some work to do at the Countway Medical Library in the morning—reviewing some reference material for my book on disability. I was also thinking about making a stop at the Coop at the corner of Brookline and Longwood to buy a compass, but I wasn't sure whether they would have one. A compass is a valuable tool for a hike, not only in the country but also in the city. As I mentioned, the streets in Downtown Boston are circular, so a compass is handy to have for that locale, but less important in Back Bay, which has a grid-like layout.

The Chestnut Hill T station was very quiet as it was early morning. The chill in the air was accentuated on the one hand by the absence of sunlight in the early morning hour and diminished on the other because the T station is below street level. Some shelter was provided by the covered waiting area. I wore a flannel long-sleeved shirt and a sweater, and I knew that the temperature would rise as the sun climbed in the sky. The parking lot was mostly empty, and the wind was fairly strong, blowing the leaves about in all directions. Occasional gusts would lift the leaves into the air, and they would swirl about before finding a landing point. In a closed environment the wind tends to bounce off solid objects like the stone partition separating the grounds of the Chestnut Hill School from the parking lot for the T.

The birds had departed from Chestnut Hill, and their music in spring and summer was a memory replaced by the stillness of autumn, broken only by the sound of the leaves rustling in the trees, the scraping of the leaves across the ground and the occasional noises of vehicles on the roads above. The only sign of animal life I could detect were some squirrels scampering about in the neighborhood looking for acorns and chestnuts. And what a joy it is to see a squirrel standing on its hind legs holding an acorn in its front paws!

As luck would have it, the inbound train came about ten minutes after I arrived, and I was on my way. The train pulled out of the station rather slowly, and I was lucky to have the chance to examine the vegetation on both sides of the T tracks. Access to the tracks from the adjacent land is blocked by barbed wire fencing, alongside of which are bushes and small trees. After a full two seasons of growth, they looked wild and woolly and in need of trimming. The area is difficult to access to a certain extent, but nevertheless it requires maintenance.

The train gradually picked up speed, and it became much more difficult to get any focus on the places beyond the fences that were still close by such as a tree in a backyard or the back of a garage. However, more distant structures could be easily delineated and you could actually see many details, such as state of repair, of various structures, buildings, roofs, fences and backyard items. A ride on the T tends to be very smooth and quiet—jostling and noises are not significant. The moving train opened good views of the trees of Brookline. The trees were fewer in number and much more isolated across the wide expanses that came into view than their counterparts in Newton, but they too showed a brilliant flush of color.

The train stopped at various stations along the route, and I was hardly conscious of the stops as the surroundings captured my attention. The ride was pleasant, and it was not long before the train was pulling out of Brookline Village and heading through the Riverway to my first destination, the Longwood Avenue T station

The Longwood T station is at street level and lets passengers out at Chapel Street. But Chapel Street is at a low point there, and a walk up that street toward Longwood involves a fairly steep ascent. I walked along the border of the Riverway, and there was plenty of shade from the street maples, which had very rich autumn colors. At the corner of Longwood I turned left and walked across the bridge over the T and continued on the north side of the block. I very rarely crossed Longwood to walk on the south side of the street, and indeed most of the foot traffic is on the T side of the street. I walked past some very young and some very ancient-looking oaks and then across the Riverway past Temple Israel, heading down Longwood past the outdoor tennis courts of Simmons College. At the corner of Longwood and Brookline Avenue, I looked across the street and then at my watch, and I understood that the Coop in the Galleria was closed, so it was not the day of the compass. I continued on Longwood past the Massachusetts College of Art and the down the road past the doctors' office building and the nurses' dormitory. Just beyond that I crossed Longwood, heading to my destination, the Countway Medical Library.

THE STAIRS TO BUILDING A

Of all the places in the area, I would say that the library was one of my favorites. It is located on the campus of Harvard Medical School near the School of Public Health on Huntington Avenue. Every trip I made to the library involved a good walk. I always entered from Longwood Avenue and took the stairs up to the elevated level next to the Sears

Building and from there I headed along the quadrangle to Building A. However, when I got to the stairs of that building for my destination, there was an obstruction. The stairs are nicely proportioned and bring you up to the entrance to the building and you can walk sideways along those stairs and get to the Countway. However, there are more direct ways to get to the library. Climbing the stairs to about the level of the entrance and turning around uncovers very nice vistas to the northeast including the Fenway, the Fens, and Cambridge in the distance. After a little exploration, I found a convenient way to bypass the stairs. Those stairs can be treacherous in winter as they become covered with ice. There is a story about a former dean of the medical school, Dr. George Berry Packer, that I always found inspiring. In the winter, Dr. Packer was often seen with a shovel in hand, clearing snow and ice from the steps. It teaches us that education begins and continues with basics, and some of the best teaching is done by example.

At the library, I worked with its computer system to retrieve references for my book. At the time, computer retrieval of references was a great challenge on a personal computer but the library was up to date with its system for maintaining references. I needed to review the references as well. I always saw students in the library, reading journals and books or studying for their course work. The library has a very fine collection of medical journals and books. Some of the books are over a hundred years old.

What if a student asked me how I would explain the importance of a library in a person's education? The question seems so basic that at first blush, most people would hesitate to ask it. They would say the library's main purpose is to provide information. I would say no, there is more to it than that. The library is not only a repository of knowledge contained in writings, journals, and books, it is also a marketplace of ideas. The challenge for the student is to learn to recognize that some of those ideas are original while many are not; some of the ideas are correct, but many are incorrect; some are inspired and some mundane. Just because something appears in print does not assure its validity or quality. That is one of the major lessons for the student in the marketplace of ideas—discerning quality of information, in theory and practice. In the realm of medical science, it is essential that the reader develop this skill when evaluating method and results.

Another important lesson is that the information gained through reading various types of literature should be put to use to improve quality of life for the reader and society. Most information has practical importance. The challenge for the student is to use the information to improve personal understanding, practice, and enrich experience. Knowledge has no meaning if it does not influence method. Always be receptive to new ideas and the possibility of change. Also, the library experience is a very personal matter; each person has likes and dislikes, and there often is no consensus about a given idea or set of ideas. But most important, it is for the person to utilize the information to good advantage. And in some instances some information gained will serve as a stepping-stone for developing new ideas, methods, and inventions.

As I was completing my work at the library, I was also thinking about my itinerary after that. I walked to the Huntington Avenue T via Longwood, past Harvard Dental School and the pharmacy on the corner. I was going inbound and my destination was Copley Square, only a few stops eastward. The Huntington Avenue Green Line heading inbound doesn't enter Back Bay until it comes to Symphony station at Massachusetts Avenue. The next inbound stop is Museum of Fine Arts adjacent to the Fenway.

THE BOSTON MUSEUM OF FINE ARTS

Although I didn't plan to visit the museum, my thoughts were directed to it, likely because it was one of the stations in route to my destination and because of my fondness for the place. The Museum of Fine Arts moved from its building facing Copley Square to its new location near the Fenway in 1909. Some of my favorite paintings in the museum include those of George and Martha Washington by Gilbert Stuart in the nooks to the side above the stairs, and the works of Claude Monet, the French impressionist painter. Monet's paintings came to mind that day amid the flush of colors in the autumn leaves. He produced multiple renditions of water lilies in a pond near his home in Giverny in the style of the impressionist painters. I like the subtleties of color, fluidity of form, presentation of the natural environment under the effects of sunlight at various times of the day. There is strong thematic unity as it is the same pond described from different visual perspectives. His paintings are very large and mostly horizontally displayed. Among all his plein air paintings, the ones of scenes near his home are clearly the best designed and executed, reflecting the artist's profound attachment to nature and remarkable invention. He was a prolific painter, and he painted about 250 paintings called *Water Lilies*, many depicting the same scene at different hours of the day, and at the time the paintings were relatively inexpensive. A Boston collector of that period who was fond of Monet's work acquired many of them at an attractive price. Those paintings were subsequently donated to the Museum of Fine Arts for display to the public. There is a general and simple rule that seems applicable—the assortment of paintings in any given museum depends mostly on the price the collectors in the area would pay for paintings at the time.

Outside the Museum of Fine Arts stands Cyrus Dallin's sculpture of an Indian chief on a horse. The bronze work, sculpted in 1909, is titled *Appeal to the Great Spirit* and depicts an Indian chief from the Sioux tribe looking upward to the heavens with arms and hands in supplicative pose. The sculptor grew up in Utah and was familiar with the Ute Indians who lived there. He specialized in Indian themes. The statue is a remarkably impressive work, conveying a profound message with a religious motif that symbolizes the Native American heritage in the North America.

SYMPHONY HALL, BOSTON

Symphony was the next T stop en route to Copley Square. Symphony Hall in Boston is located at the corner of Massachusetts and Huntington Avenues, and it was built in the Renaissance style in 1900. It is the permanent home of the Boston Symphony Orchestra and the Boston Pops. Its predecessor, the Boston Music Hall, located downtown on Winter Street and Hamilton Place, was built in 1852 and served as the home of the orchestra for almost fifty years. However, at the turn of the century, there was a lot of subway and other construction in the area and the orchestra, like many other institutions, moved to Back Bay. It was not only the construction that prompted the move, it was the prospect of a brighter future in the new location. Many illustrious musicians have served in the symphony orchestra and the Pops, and the institutions have had a long history of fine musical accomplishments. As the Symphony station is in the Back Bay, this is an opportunity to discuss the neighborhood's development particularly in the area traversed by the inbound E train.

BACK BAY IN MODERN TIMES

In order to understand Back Bay present and past, one has to keep in mind that the area is not a monolith. Most descriptions emphasize its residential character with its quaint architectural patterns in the context of historical preservation. That is a limited perspective that ignores the dynamism of the area. In reality, it is a very diversified and vibrant combination of elements, residential, commercial and public real estate.

Back Bay of today is more like a city than a neighborhood, with development constantly unfolding and the community benefitting from its multifaceted character. Architecture is only one feature of Back Bay—there is much more to the community. It is what's in the buildings, and it's the human transactions that occur in the area that should get most of the attention, not the externality—the particular architectural style that they feature. For example, we can compare the Museum of Fine Arts building to a box with pleasant wrapping that contains a gift—a sampling of the world of art. It's not the box itself that is important but rather the gift within that should draw our attention. In a similar vein, Symphony Hall has an interesting exterior design but most people go there to hear music, not to admire the architecture of the building. They may do that as well, but it is not their primary objective.

Back Bay of today has separate, well-demarcated residential and commercial areas. In contrast, in its early days in the late 1800s after the marshes of the area were filled, the area was mostly a residential enclave. It subsequently witnessed commercial development mostly in its southern section, along Newbury and Boylston streets and Huntington Avenue.

Perusing a map of the area, most residents of the areas outside Boston observe that all roads appear to lead to Boston. Historically, however, the roads actually started in Boston and fanned out in a westerly direction in the path of urban development. So, for example, Huntington Avenue originated from its intersection with Boylston Street. But in considering how streets enter Boston, we note that Huntington Avenue originates at the Jamaicaway as a continuation of the Boylston Streets of Newton and Brookline and enters Back Bay obliquely, ending just short of Boylston Street at Saint James Street in Boston. Commercial enterprises, small and large, located themselves along those streets, which traverse the neighborhood from west to east. The breadth of the commercial streets, particularly in certain central areas, tends to be typical of most avenues,

COMMERCIAL DEVELOPMENT IN BACK BAY

Commercial development began early in the history of Back Bay. Starting about 1880, various businesses located first, on Boylston Street, and then, at the turn of the century, on Newbury Street. The businesses were very small and specialized, consisting of apparel vendors, art galleries, and similar retail businesses that could be accommodated in the small commercial buildings which often were recycled from residential structures. The vendors would use space by creating a below-ground level and also second and third floors as the space had height but little depth and width. Department stores first appeared in the early 1900s and were located mostly Downtown. A few, however, found their way into Back Bay. The major additions in that area came with the development of the Prudential Center (the Pru) in 1964 and then Copley Place in 1983, each a multipurpose commercial development, featuring fashionable retail stores and high-class office space. Copley Place also has hotels and is connected to the Pru by a glass-enclosed skywalk over Huntington Avenue.

COPLEY SQUARE AREA: A HISTORICAL EPICENTER OF BACK BAY

My designated starting point for a walking tour of the commercial side of Back Bay was the Copley Square area, and Copley was the next T stop. Copley Square is an area in Back Bay that is bustling with activity and is rich in history. It is not only the square but the buildings and streets nearby that reflect much of the vibrancy and the history of the area. In order to appreciate Copley Square, you have understand that it is a product of eclecticism, a mélange of disparate elements that are at times distracting, so it is best to dissect the principal elements and focus on those. We will review Copley Square present in the context of Copley Square past to provide a better understanding of the development of the area.

The Copley Square station lets out just adjacent to the Boston Public Library located on the south side of Boylston Street between Exeter and Dartmouth streets. The original Boston Public Library was built in 1895.

A mixture of new and old buildings is found on the opposite side of Boylston Street between Exeter and Dartmouth. At the northeast corner of Boylston and Exeter is a modern office building that has a horizontal predisposition with interesting architectural features. The fifteen-story building at 699 Boylston Street was designed by Jung Brannen Associates and built in 1968. Its design was way ahead of its time and has been nicknamed the "Darth Vader" building after the Star Wars character. It has an interesting color motif—green windows and accentuating panels with light pink concrete mixed side by side. The windows project in some places giving them the appearance of bay windows. The building also has a tapering top that is not easily seen from the street.

As you walk toward Dartmouth Street, you can see older buildings that, unlike One Exeter Place, which was designed for commercial use, look like they were originally residential structures that were converted to commercial use. The entire Back Bay started as a residential area, and the two streets to the south of Commonwealth Avenue then saw commercial development. The first floors have display windows, and the building setbacks are quite large. The sidewalk is large enough to accommodate box planters and fairly sizable bush planters at the edge of the street. The street trees in the area are London plane trees, *Platanus acerifolia*, and the scientific name derives from the shield-like appearance of the leaf and its resemblance to a maple leaf. In the fall the leaves turn from green to yellow. The bark of those trees is mostly peeling, disclosing a mottled greenish-brown pattern.

At the northwest corner of Dartmouth and Boylston streets stands the Old South Church designed by Cummings and Sears and built in 1873. The Congregationalist church moved from the Old South Meeting House Downtown. It has a very special heritage as many of the American patriots belonged to that church. Many of the churches relocated to Back Bay from Downtown and some even earlier. The Old South Church was established in 1669, organized by Congregationalist dissenters from Boston's First Church. Its first home was Cedar Meeting House from 1670 to 1730. It then moved to Old South Meeting House and remained there until 1875. The church in Back Bay has various other names including New Old South Church and Third Church.

The architectural style is Venetian gothic, and when you look at the building, you get the impression that it belongs on a hillside in a bucolic setting. However, in its current location, the large structure with high and low elements side by side seems constrained in such a crowded urban space. Its exterior is ornate and cheerful with a tall bell tower, or campanile, that dominates the structure's presentation. The building has exterior brown walls made of Roxbury puddingstone. The stones have various darker and lighter shades. The presentation is dressed up, and the colors in the brownstone walls and the roofs with red and black slate tiles and the green cupola attract added interest. From the time it was built until 1915, the bell tower was the tallest structure in the area, reaching a height of 246 feet. That tower could be seen from many locations in Back Bay and even from Downtown. However, the siting of the church in Back Bay's filled-in marshes did cause some architectural instability in the tower. The top-heavy bell tower did not have adequate support in the pilings that were driven into the ground and fill of Back Bay. The campanile, which houses a two-ton bell, started to list to one side in about the 1920s and had to be replaced.

BOSTON PUBLIC LIBRARY

The municipal library in Boston, called the Boston Public Library, was founded in 1848. It has a commanding presence in the Copley Square area just to the west of the square. It has one of the largest collections of books and digital media in the country. In the collection are more than 1.7 million rare books and manuscripts. The Boston Public Library has an active circulation about 3.7 million items annually. It initially opened in 1854 on Mason Street with 16,000 volumes. After four years, it moved into a larger building fronting on Boylston Street. It moved to its current location in approximately 1888. The library building was modeled after the Bibliotheque Nationale of Paris in the Renaissance style, designed by architect Charles Follen McKim. A large annex was built to the west of the building, so the library occupies most of the Boylston Street south side between Dartmouth and Exeter streets.

THE ORIGIN OF COPLEY SQUARE

It is a truism that all squares originate in vacant land, as do buildings. In its early history, a portion of Copley Square of today was a vacant lot, the site that Trinity Church was built on. As the lot was triangular, the square actually started out as a triangle, and in its evolution that triangle was looking for a similarly shaped triangle to complete the square—or more precisely, the rectangle. Photographs taken at the time the church was built show that the neighboring Back Bay to the south was mostly empty. The area had been filled in, but there was much vacant space.

A city square is defined as an open area bounded on four sides by streets. In urban areas, it often is a landscaped area that is used as a park or memorial. More often than not it has the shape of a rectangle. Copley Square of today is enclosed by four streets, Dartmouth Street to the west, Boylston Street to the north, Clarendon Street to the east and Saint James Street to the south. Historically, Copley Square started out as a triangle, as Huntington Avenue formerly bisected the square. Once Huntington Avenue was recircuited to connect with Saint James Street rather than Boylston Street, the rectangular shape of the square was restored. With that understanding, it is clear that the only occupant of Copley Square is Trinity Church. The Museum of Fine Arts at the corner of Saint James and Dartmouth Streets opened in 1876, and it was not in Copley Square but faced it. Other buildings in the area are in the vicinity of the square but outside of it.

Trinity Church in Copley Square was designed by the architect Henry Hobson Richardson and built between 1872 and 1877 for an Episcopalian congregation that lost its church on Summer Street in Downtown in the great fire of 1872. The building had an excellent location, in that it was off Boylston but not far from it. One great advantage was that the lot permitted the construction of a west-facing building that was not constrained by a corner location and could be easily seen from blocks away. The architecture is Romanesque, somewhat austere in character, with a very impressive and formal frontal presentation with great visual impact. The architect used a balanced and focused presentation of elements with a rich brown color and heavy arches. There is a front element with pyramid-shaped roofs to either side, and atop the roof of the adjacent structure is a massive tower, also appointed with a pyramidal roof. There are small columns with cone-shaped pediments in the upper portion, a design reminiscent of a medieval castle. There is another much smaller parish building on the right side of the church.

There was a flurry of building activity in Boston at about the time of the centennial of the independence of our nation. The building in the Copley Square area started with the building of Trinity Church the year before the centennial year. Then there was major construction that changed the character of the entire area, the building of the Museum of Fine Arts at the corner of Saint James and Dartmouth streets, which occurred in 1876. It added a major cultural attraction to the neighborhood that had a strong impact. When the museum arrived, the square was called Art Square until 1883, when the name was changed to Copley

Square, after the Boston portrait artist John Singleton Copley of the era of the American Revolution. The museum gave the square its identity, and it was the main public cultural focus. Hence, it is a profound irony that the square lost the museum as a tenant after another large public institution was built next to it in the late 1800s.

THE MUSEUM OF FINE ARTS: A CENTRAL ELEMENT IN COPLEY SQUARE DEPARTS

The old Museum of Fine Arts had a great location in Back Bay, and it had many years of success until a new development occurred that seemed to preordain its departure. The building of the library across the street most likely was the factor that prompted its relocation. The two elements were incompatible, and the city planners should have realized that. Trying to place two very large and different public institutions side by side reflected a profound lapse in urban planning and to try to place two very large and different public institutions side by side showed an even a more extreme lack of social understanding.

When it comes to neighborhoods, a public library, no matter how distinguished is the institution or the building it is in, does not belong next to a museum of fine arts. Each institution has its individuality and importance. Obviously Boston needed both a first-class museum of fine arts and a first-class public library; however, it is also clear that they do not belong adjacent to one another. There are many other considerations that would argue against such an ill-conceived juxtaposition. For example, a museum benefits from tranquil surroundings but a library draws large crowds and sees heavy daily use. Sadly, one of the consequences of the forced departure of the Museum of Fine Arts was the loss of the magnificent building it was in, which was subsequently destroyed.

COPLEY SQUARE TODAY

Today, Copley Square has a park area within it. The square also has adjacent buildings, including the John Hancock Tower and the Fairmont Copley Plaza Hotel. The Boston Public Library is across the street on Dartmouth and Boylston. The development in Copley Square shows a slightly uncomfortable mixture and arrangement of elements. On the one hand, there is a church over a century old and on the other a modern skyscraper that is tilted to one direction to gain attention, detracting attention from the church. It is an interesting conundrum having dissimilar elements in such a small space. Obviously each deserves its own place under the sun. However, together in their current location they give the impression of disorderliness and tension arising from their heterogeneity and proximity. Nevertheless, we can summarize the principal elements as a church, a skyscraper, and a hotel, and a library and another church across the street. Distinguished by its absence is the Museum of Fine Arts, which had opened in the centennial year 1876 but moved to a new location near the Fenway in the early 1900s.

SKYSCRAPERS IN BACK BAY

A very surprising development in the history of Back Bay, a Boston neighborhood, was the building of skyscrapers. Ordinarily one would expect skyscrapers to be located in the downtown area, not in the midst of a mostly residential area like Back Bay. The first tall building to be built in the area was the Prudential Tower, known as the Pru, which was built by the Prudential Insurance Company in 1964 near the intersection of Huntington Avenue and West Newton Street. It was built as an urban renewal project that involved construction of a shopping center with the skyscraper office building in the center. It reaches a height of 749 feet, making it the seventy-seventh tallest building in the United States. At the time it was built, it was the tallest building in both Boston and New England, surpassing the Custom House Tower built in 1915, which reaches 496 feet.

THE JOHN HANCOCK TOWER: ONE OF THREE JOHN HANCOCK BUILDINGS IN BOSTON

In Back Bay of today, there are three adjacent buildings each called the John Hancock Building. For simplicity's sake, these are presented in order of the time of their building and termed John Hancock buildings one, two, and three. The first, built in 1922, is the Stephen L. Brown Building at 197 Clarendon Street, designed by Parker, Thomas & Rice. John Hancock number two, built in 1947 at 200 Berkeley Street—also called the Berkeley Building—was designed by Cram and Ferguson. It stands behind John Hancock number one, and it was the tallest building built in the city in the 1940s. John Hancock number three, built in 1976 at 200 Clarendon Street and designed by the architect Henry Cobb of I. M. Pei & Associates, is the tower building, which is sixty stories high—it has the shape of a cereal box. It became the tallest building in the area, reaching 790 feet in height. It features a reflective blue-glass design in which you can see the environment around it, including nearby and faraway buildings and even the clouds in the sky. Both buildings one and two are seen in this building's reflection.

THE ADVANTAGES AND DISADVANTAGES OF A NORTHEAST EXPOSURE

One of the interesting points emphasized by this building is that in the beginning of the 1970s, the area had been developed and land for construction was not readily available. So the place chosen for the tower was actually a secondary site along Clarendon Street away from the more central location of Copley Square. To compensate for the location, the building was constructed angulated to the northeast rather than facing directly east. There are several noteworthy advantages to that spatial orientation of the building. First, this permits its frontal presentation to be seen from the more central areas in Back Bay and from Downtown as well. Second, the reflective blue glass glistens in the sunlight, and its color fits in well against a blue sky. The light blue is an excellent choice as it tends to capture attention in the environment. Also, the color provides better contrast than would a light green, for example. Moreover, glass is perfect for a narrow box-like structure. The reflective properties permit a variety of images to be seen in the building's exterior. You can see many scenes, depending on the vantage point and the view that the specific part of the building reflects. There are different images on lower levels than on higher levels. This makes the building a major visual center of attraction in Back Bay.

On the other hand, there are also disadvantages to the orientation of the building not perceived by the architect or the builders, and the main one involves the stability of the structure in a strong wind. After its construction was completed and tenants occupied the building, it experienced serious technical difficulties related to the force of the winds from the northeast.

A BATTLE BETWEEN NATURE AND A SKYSCRAPER: THE WINDS VERSUS THE WINDOWS

In autumn in coastal New England, the winds come from the northeast. Low atmospheric pressure areas form offshore in the Atlantic. Starting in Canada and New England, they have a rotation center north of Boston off the upper New England coast. The leading winds in the left forward quadrant sweep across the mainland from the northeast. Boston is among the windiest cities in the United States with an average wind speed of 12.3 miles per hour. As winter approaches, the wind speed increases, reaching 13.4 miles per hour, which is about 42 percent higher than in the rest of the country. The record wind speed recorded in the area is 31.3 miles per hour.

When winds strike skyscrapers, they cause sway—that is, the building is actually moved by the wind. A slight sway usually goes unnoticed, but it varies, and a person on one of the upper floors can actually feel the rocking of the building in the wind when the sway is strong. It is like driving a car on a highway with the winds striking the vehicle from one side or the other—there is a feeling of sway with any size vehicle, but more prominent in smaller and lighter cars. With respect to the John Hancock Tower, tenants noticed the sway in the upper floors and there was no mistake as to the cause. Then the windows blew out. In the early days of the structure it was common to see boards covering the blown out windows. The windows were smashed because of several factors. First, the building faces northeast–southwest instead of east–west, as you would expect. The winds come from the northeast, and their full force is applied to the building. There is no other building in the area that faces northeast; all face east–west, including the Prudential Tower. Also, when the building is very tall it catches the higher, stronger winds. In addition, a wide glass design also tends to trap the wind, while a tall and narrow design escapes it.

The windows blew out regularly and had to be boarded up, and the building had to be shut down. The existing windows were replaced with stronger glass windows but that was not sufficient. It was not until large shock absorbers were installed below the building to help it resist wind-induced sway that the problem was corrected. When that was done, the sway diminished, and the windows held.

PARK SQUARE

The walking route down Boylston Street to Park Square takes you through a commercial area that is a mixture of ongoing development and historical preservation. The street trees change—littleleaf lindens replace the London planes. The New England Life Insurance building is located at 501 Boylston Street between Clarendon and Berkeley streets. It features an art deco style and a tower that is not seen from street level. A short distance from there is Park Square, an area with a long history in Boston that has seen many changes. Park Square is formed by the intersection of Charles Street on the east, Stuart Street on the south, Arlington Street on the west, and Boylston Street on the north. The square developed into an important commercial site for businesses and hotels starting in the second quarter of the 1800s. The earliest commerce developed around the railroad station, called the Park Square Station, which was located at the northeastern corner of the square. The railroad was a major impetus to the development of Back Bay. The square had bordering areas with theaters and night clubs to the east between Boylston Street and Tremont Street.

PARK SQUARE IN THE TWENTIETH CENTURY: FROM RAGS TO RICHES

Park Square was a commercial area with a populist character. It was the embodiment of a commercial area that offered promise to small and large retail enterprises. Many of the businesses were owned by immigrants, who had come to this country in search of economic opportunities. There were stores with general appeal and also hotels, bars, nightclubs, and theaters. In the early days of development in Back Bay, commercial enterprises, largely retail, started on a very small scale. The buildings were mixed-use: first floor commercial and upper stories residential. In commercial areas, many of the buildings of the early times displayed mostly a residential character, not dissimilar to the brownstones in other parts of Back Bay. The entire area, however, tended to be on the seedy side, as if the foreboding spirit of the southern side of

Boston Common spilled over into the adjacent neighborhood. It was redeemed to a significant extent in 1927 by the new and hopeful construction of a luxury hotel, the Statler, built in the center of the square by the hotelier Henry Statler.

Since 1927, the inner portion of Park Square has been occupied by a luxury hotel and a parking garage. The art deco–style hotel is located on a triangular-shaped lot, and it has a unique triangular shape. The building across the street is a parking garage, also constructed in art deco style, with various commercial tenants on the ground floor facing the street. The garage lobby, decorated with an art deco interior pattern makes it quite unusual for a garage. Those two buildings and other art deco buildings on Arlington Street have dominated the square since that time. The area was upgraded at about the time of the bicentennial with two buildings along Boylston Street facing the Public Garden—a condominium building and the Four Seasons Hotel.

Outside the limits of Park Square, but very close by to the east, is the theater district enclosed by Boylston and Tremont streets and to the south, a bar and nightclub district between Stuart and Melrose Streets. The Cocoanut Grove nightclub was just south of the square at 17 Piedmont. It was a single floor structure with a large dining room, dance floor, and stage; the roof could be opened in the summer. It was established in 1927 during the Roaring Twenties. It was the place of dreams, of tropical delights, a landmark in the city. During the early 1940s, in particular, the Grove was the place to go. On Saturday evening November 28, 1942, when the club was packed with an estimated one thousand patrons, a flash fire erupted. The building had at least one boarded-up exit, poorly marked exits, and an exit with an inward-opening door. There was only one usable exit, a revolving entrance door, which got jammed as patrons attempted to flee. There was no firefighting paraphernalia in the building, and five alarms were sent to the fire department. The blaze spread like wildfire, and in less than an hour the dream nightclub of an entire Boston generation was destroyed. The flames and smoke and the stampede of fleeing patrons claimed the lives of 490 people, and injured 166 people. It was the worst nightclub fire in American history and one of the most painful memories in the city's modern history.

There were many lessons learned from that tragic fire, and although five are highlighted here there are undoubtedly many more. First, overcrowding of any facility creates a host of hazards. Second, exits must be clearly marked and conducive to the flow of people fleeing from danger. Third, the use of flammable materials in the interior of buildings should be avoided. Fourth, electrical circuitry of all buildings is to be carefully inspected and maintained. Finally, there must be firm resolve to correct the problems and then move on. It makes no sense to try to sweep history under the rug to shield people from painful memories. When that particularly important lesson in history is learned, a new Cocoanut Grove, bigger and better, will be built and the lost dreams of an earlier generation will be recaptured by a new generation.

PARK SQUARE AT THE TIME OF THE BICENTENNIAL

In approximately 1976, Boylston Street between Arlington and Charles Streets had an eclectic group of buildings dating from the late 1800s that faced the Public Garden. They were typical of buildings on the street at the time with mixed commercial and residential use. At the time, it was much more popular to photograph the northern side of Boylston Street, which borders on the Public Garden, than the southern side. Boylston Street at that time was much quieter than it is today. Horse and carriage and trolley transportation were in use at the time and the traffic pattern was different. Arlington Street ended at Boylston Street in those days. There was a trolley that entered the park from Boylston Street just east of Arlington Street.

AUTUMN IN BOSTON

Nature's cycles unfold throughout the year according to various patterns and schedules. We call periods that see annual changes in the earth's climate and the geophysical environment the "seasons," arising as a consequence of the tilting of the planet toward or away from the sun in earth's annual orbit around the sun. Living forms adapt to those changes, but not necessarily in the same way. Each form of life has its own patterns and rhythms in adapting to the climatic changes.

In the summer in the Northeast in general and in New England in particular, there is an exodus of people from urban areas to the mountains and seashore, so the Public Garden and the city tend to be quiet. However, despite the relative scarcity of people, there is plenty of activity. Birds for example, flock to the place in summer. The lagoon attracts visiting birds such as ducks and Canada geese. The dove is also a frequent visitor. The small musical birds are visitors of spring and summer, and they favor the branches of leafy trees. They are elusive, rarely seen unless they draw the viewer's attention with their musical calls. Their music is so different from the music we are accustomed to. Their calls are usually a very short, high-pitched passage that soars over the stillness. It is repeated over and over again and generally only stops when the bird flies to a different location. The music of birds consists mostly of stillness punctuated by a short musical tattoo. The music of humans is the opposite, with virtually continuous melodic passages and very little intervening stillness. Among the instruments of the orchestra the ones that have the sound range closest to that of the birds are the woodwinds. The flute and piccolo, in particular, have remarkable capacity to mimic the higher tones of the birds. The string instruments, in contrast, are great for mimicking the sounds of the winds and seas. For birds, the change of season from summer to fall signals the end of their visit to the area. They generally migrate to warmer areas in the south. So, in autumn, when the Public Garden birds have departed, their summer music is only a recent memory. Autumn is also a busy season for the northeastern gray squirrel. The cool air and falling leaves seem to be signals that winter is not far off. And with acorns and chestnuts falling from the trees, there is a flurry of activity by the squirrel to gather autumn's bounty for use in winter. With the gray squirrel preoccupied in autumn, we can try to meet a great challenge of balance in nature: finding the few red squirrels left in the area among the gray squirrel predominance.

For man, autumn is a season of annual beginnings: return to school and work after the recreational pursuits of summer. It is a time of fixing and planting, as well. In the fall in the Northeast, man-made structures have to be repaired and secured so that they can withstand the severe weather of winter. The heat-stressed grass of summer has to be reseeded so that it will grow in the spring. And in the fall, the flowers of spring are planted.

We feel the cycles of nature with our senses. Certain cycles are perceived by auditory sensations. When the autumn weather arrives, the songbirds leave the area, giving rise to an eerie stillness in nature. The music of spring and summer suddenly disappears, as the birds fly southward. The silence in nature is replaced by a spectacular visual display and a very significant change in the temperature. The leaves change color, and the warmth of summer is replaced by the chill of autumn. The winds strengthen in the fall, and they are an important factor in the descent of the leaves in that season. So at various times in autumn, the splash of color in the Public Garden is either in the treetops, on the ground, or swirling about in the wind.

A WALK IN THE PUBLIC GARDEN IN AUTUMN

Occasionally, a walk in the Public Garden in autumn can be compared to a particular and exceptionally good hand in poker—a royal flush.

Trees may be just at the right point in revealing the brilliance of their colors, and the weather and time of day may be very favorable for viewing the display. On the Boylston Street side of the park, the elms and maples dominate with their spectacular yellows and reds. Views from various vantage points of a stand of trees tend to be very impressive. A flush of color is a powerful sign of autumn in the park. The tops of the elms reveal a lush yellow, streaked with tinges of red. The time of day makes a difference in their appearance. Yellow is seen best in the morning, while the red is brought out best at sunset. The view to the west is the view to the setting sun. Images of the trees are reflected in the lagoon. The waters in the man-made lagoon tend to be very quiet, and there are generally no ripples seen on the surface. This makes the reflective power of the body of water even greater, with less distortion of the reflected images. The time of the month during which the amazing flush of color is present is variable. A few cold and windy days can hasten the fall of the leaves from the trees and shorten the duration of the spectacular show of leaves in the Public Garden.

PUBLIC GARDEN TREES IN AUTUMN

Maples are very common trees throughout the Northeast. They thrive in areas with a temperate climate, tending to establish themselves rather easily and grow rapidly, especially in the higher elevations. There are many varieties of the tree, and the maples are easily recognized by their leaves and trunks. Their leaves are shaped like a hand, with five angular projections of varying sizes and are arranged one opposite the other on the stem. Park maples are of three varieties: the Norway maple, silver maple, and red maple. Each of these types has palmate leaves that are green in the spring and summer. In autumn, however, the former two have leaves that turn bright yellow, while the latter types of leaves first turn yellow and then brilliant scarlet.

The Boylston side of the park has mostly Norway maples, *Acer platanoides*, and red maples, *Acer rubrum*. Norway maples tend to have very small hand-like leaves that have small pointed projections as if the fingers of the hand are closed. The Beacon Street side has silver maples, *Acer saccharinum*, which have larger and wider leaves and very sharply defined digit-like projections, as if the fingers of the hand are spread out. The leaves of *Acer rubrum* are generously proportioned, also with distinct pointed projections. For some reason, the Japanese maple, *Acer palmatum*, was not included in the original plantings. One variety of that tree, called "fireglow," has maroon leaves with a palmate leaf with stellate form like a starfish. The tree is a diminutive one and a very slow grower, and perhaps that was the reason that it was not included. However, it would provide some color in spring and summer in the otherwise sea of green in the treetops of the maples and most other trees.

The family of beech trees is easily identified by the large gray trunk with smooth bark; the branches that generally grow downward, covering the trunk; and the leaves, which have an oval shape like elm leaves but tend to be more rounded. The trunk often has the appearance of multiple trunks fused together. The park beeches are also of three types: the purple beech, *Fagus purpurea*, which has a large smooth trunk and drooping purple leaves. Those are located adjacent to the entrance on the Arlington Street side of the park and also along the main walkway through the center of the park leading to Charles Street. Another type, the European beech, *Fagus sylvatica*, is located in various places one at the Arlington Street side and two in the northeast corner of the park. Lastly, the weeping European beech, *Fagus sylvatica pendula*, is found on either side of the central walkway. A fully grown weeping European beech is a sight to behold, as it looks like an upside-down tree with branches that are heavy with leaves, extending downward and covering the trunk completely. Its appearance suggests that the tree is growing downward instead of upward and from a distance it looks like a manmade, tent-like shelter.

The elms in the public garden are generally very large trees, and most are located along the walking path at the Boylston Street side of the park. An elm can be identified by its gray trunk with a wavy bark pattern; its branches, which are eccentrically located, pointing laterally and often drooping; and its leaves, oval in shape with serrated edges. There are six types of elms in the park: American elm, *Ulmus Americana*; Belgian elm, *Ulmus hollandica "Belgica"*; Camperdown elm, *Ulmus glabra tricuspida*; English elm, *Ulmus procera*; Rock elm, *Ulmus thomasii*; and Scotch elm, *Ulmus glabra*. The first three types of elm tree are located along the Boylston Street side of the park and the other three are in the northern half of the park. The elm leaves turn a bright yellow in the fall and their color is accentuated by sunlight during the day and streetlamps at night.

Oak trees are tall hardwoods that have a commanding presence in the park as they do elsewhere in the Northeast, with rough bark on very straight trunks and with hand-shaped leaves that turn from green to a lustrous copper hue in the fall. There are only three types of oaks in the park with either pointed or rounded edged leaves: the Pin oak, *Quercus palustris* (pointed); the Burr oak, *Quercus macrocarpa* (rounded); and the English oak, *Quercus robur* (rounded). There is one of each in the various quadrants of the park: a Pin oak in the Boylston Street–Arlington Street area, a Burr oak, also in the Beacon Street–Arlington Street area, and an English oak in the Beacon Street–Charles Street area.

The willows of the park, located around the lagoon at the waterside edge, are deciduous trees with drooping branches; small, narrow oval leaves; and deeply fissured bark. The term weeping willow, *Salix Babylonica*, likely derives from the Bible, from the writing in Psalms: "By the waters of Babylon, there we sat and wept, when we remembered Zion." The willow trees in the Public Garden are of a common northeastern variety of weeping willow, *S. pendulina* "*elegantissima.*" Graceful trees, they provide a counterpoint in fall, as their leaves often remain green when those of the other broadleaves are yellow and red. Leaves of the willows bloom later in spring and last longer in autumn than do those of the other broadleaf trees in the park. Weeping willows are pyramidal in shape with a conical crown, and they reach a height of about thirty to forty feet at maturity, with a spread of about thirty-five feet.

The trees in the park may come from large well-known families, such as the elms, maples, beeches, and oaks, and when they do, they often have a sizable representation, or they may come from smaller lesser-known families and may be present as single trees in the park. The latter variety includes the Pagoda tree, *Sophora japonica*, which is located in the northwest quadrant of the park. Another type of tree that has but a few examples in the park is the horse chestnut tree, *Aesculus hippocastanum*, which can grow to considerable height with an impressive canopy of leaves. Its bark is gray and fairly smooth, and its leaves are arranged in clusters in a fanlike pattern. The individual leaf resembles that of the elm, but the pointed edge is oriented to the center, and the rounded wide edge faces the outside. Chestnuts are a typical constituent of this tree.

The Japanese larch tree, *Larix kaempferi*, another unusual tree, is a deciduous conifer. The tree has a golden tone in the fall. Its branches are horizontal and rarely droop. Like other conifers, it has pinecones. Its leaves turn yellow and red in the autumn before they fall from the tree.

When the leaves fall in autumn, trees lose a major element that distinguishes them. Bare tree branches are only a temporary interlude in nature, an interlude that presages the coming of winter. In fall and the coming winter buds of new leaves are dormant until the arrival of the next spring. For the trees, autumn is a season of preparation for winter.

With the loss of the leaves, the trees being lighter, can better withstand the cold of winter, including the snow. For the leaves, autumn is their final season of the year.

WINTER IN BOSTON COMMON

When the trees are bare and the temperature drops in the fall, then winter is rapidly approaching. The days become shorter, and the sun sets earlier. As we approach the beginning of winter, which occurs on December 21, the day becomes very short and activities that can only be performed in daylight are curtailed. At the winter solstice one twenty-four-hour revolution of the earth provides only a brief exposure of the northeast to the sun, hence the shorter day. As one moves in a northerly direction the day becomes even shorter, and at the north pole there is no daylight at all, only darkness for twenty-four hours. The earth's axial tilt together with the longer distance from the sun make the northeast's exposure to the sun's rays of shorter duration on the first day of winter. The shorter and less direct exposure to the sun makes the temperatures go down, both that of the atmosphere and the surface of the earth itself.

The Common in winter loses most of its verdant color. The leaves have gone, and the grass, a lush green color in summer, becomes a light brown after in winter due to the cold. The animal life in the Common tends to be less in view as the birds have long departed for warmer areas, and the smaller animals seek refuge from the cold in places that are mostly out of sight. The harshness of winter in New England is not friendly to the natural habitat—the plants and animals tend to battle for survival in winter. Plant life is often in its most basic form, and the animals tend to seek shelter from the cold. Some hibernate. Thus, it appears that the park is in hibernation, as well. Any fault in the man-made environment, such as chips and cracks in the paved walkways and broken wooden slats in the benches, tend to attract the most attention in winter as the dormant natural environment in the park tends to be subdued.

A WALK THROUGH BOSTON COMMON ON A VERY COLD DAY

It was a clear and very cold day when I entered the Common from Charles Street and after a short walk quickly ascended to higher ground. The skyline of the city unfolded before my eyes and was sparsely punctuated by tall buildings in clusters downtown. There was not a cloud in the sky. The cold was intense; merciless and relentless January winds blew in from the northeast, sweeping across the high places in the park. There was little shelter, with the leaves long gone from the trees, leaving gaping spaces for the wind to wreak its havoc. The Common was frozen and there were few signs of life. No squirrels, no birds, and very few people were in sight. Even a fur hat, thick gloves, and a down-filled coat that reached almost to the knees were no match for the blistering cold and the winds of winter. On that day, the Common was a place to be only because it was a crossing point to another destination—Downtown. And because most direct paths from Charles Street to Tremont Street were over elevations of terrain, the walk was numbing.

On that day it seemed as if the Common was frozen in history as well. There was a strange quiet that gripped the park as if the good and evil spirits of the past were in repose. The park was a creation of nature, and it was thriving long before it was given the name Boston Common in 1634. Its character did not change with a new appellation and all of the monuments placed in the park after that pale in significance compared with the immense physical and historical presence of the site itself. The history of the site before 1634, unfortunately, is not well characterized. In contrast, the history after that is well documented, but it is mostly ignominious. Boston Common is haunted by good and evil spirits of its malevolent past—the good spirits represent the victims, and the evil spirits are those who did them harm.

It is difficult to escape the negative historical associations of Boston Common—the Boston Massacre, which occurred not in the Common of today but nearby that set the stage for the place. The Common has a checkered history of mayhem with mob violence, and a legacy of religious intolerance and superstitions. It is unclear what it was that attracted evildoers to that place. Many, of course, weren't considered in that light in their times, which is a painful irony today. But it is the oldest park in the country, and from a historical perspective they were the epitome of evil.

THE MARTYRS OF THE ECCLESIASTICAL LAWS OF THE PURITANS

The law of the Puritans was a combination of secular and religious law and infractions of either were met with public punishment. The Common was the site of public executions, including those of people shamefully persecuted by the Puritans, such as Quakers and individuals branded as practicing witchcraft. The religious intolerance that is reflected in those acts tarnishes the legacy of the Puritans to this day. The unfortunate legacies of the religious laws and governance were superstition, religious zealotism and bias, intolerance, and violence. With the birth of the nation there was an attempt to remove religious law from the laws governing our country. Emancipation from religious law has been very important in the development of our democracy. We are a nation with people of different religious backgrounds. It has been a major step forward not to allow any religious sectarianism or partisanship to influence the law or its application. Civil laws—not religious laws—govern our country. Notwithstanding, there are new laws constantly being formulated some with features that subvert the intent of the Constitution regarding separation of church and state. Or there may be interference with the application of laws based upon religious considerations. There is a history of laws that were an attempt to manipulate in that direction: the so-called blue laws. A blue law is a religious law that restricts entertainment, leisure activities, the operation of businesses, and shopping on a Sunday. Such laws date back to colonial New England and have been overturned by the courts as they are in blatant violation of the First Amendment. In the personal sphere, an individual is free to subscribe to any religious law except when that law violates the civil law. Separation of church and state is a fundamental principle of our democracy. Weakness in addressing religious discrimination in the law opens the road to weakness in dealing with other forms of discrimination—they are interrelated. Discrimination in any sphere is not consistent with the principles on which our nation was founded.

BIGOTRY IN PUBLIC FORUMS

The Common has been a site of other political and religious bigotry, as well, a popular place for hateful and demagogic tirades and diatribes proffered by individuals afforded the protection of free speech and audited by sympathizers guaranteed freedom of assembly under the Constitution. However, when it comes to bigotry in a public forum, the personal freedom to reject that evil with both hands is also guaranteed by the Constitution. All that was frozen in time that day, but the evil behind it would resurface in the memories of the place once the park thawed.

On a day like that, any blemishes or signs of disrepair of the park were masked by human distraction due to the cold. The remnants of the rank grass of summer were frozen solid. Not a single acorn from fall remained. The trees were mostly bare, and park benches with crumbling wood and aging cement bases drew no attention in the battle to traverse the park as quickly as possible. The monuments, which generally seemed well kept, had a much greater overall impact in the deep freeze of the season. On a day like that, there was no incentive to linger in the Common or to meander around Frog Pond to explore the foothills of Beacon Hill—it was too cold for any of that. There was no reason to exit the Common anywhere but in a straight line to your destination. That of course would be impossible because the eastward trek out of the Common brings you to the streets of old Boston, which twist and turn like the thread in a ball of wool after the cat played with it. And you wonder to yourself why the parking lot was adjacent to Charles Street rather than Tremont Street and why history placed a fifty-acre obstacle between you and your destination.

When the park was released from the grip of Boreus a few days later, and with general thaw caused by the moderation in temperature, you could see that the park itself was in a poor repair and overall in a neglected state. It seemed as though there was very little maintenance being done. The paths were cracking and the park benches were in poor repair. The trees badly needed trimming and overall there was a great need to reclaim the area with new trees and plantings. There was neglect in other areas of the city, as well, but in a way the disrepair in the Common seemed to be typical of that. It seemed to symbolize neglect in perpetuity, which reflects the wrong attitude. For some reason, a park of such great historical importance was permitted to deteriorate, and there was no attempt to intervene, as if there was something sacred about its shabby condition that had to be preserved. That approach may be called a common error.

PRESERVATION OF HISTORICAL PLACES EMPHASIZING FUNCTIONALITY

In modern society we are faced with important challenges in protecting the historical environment, one of the aspects of that involves protecting historical sites. In many instances the goal of preserving history comes into conflict with current environmental usage. It is important to understand that not everything from the past needs to be preserved in its original form. There is a natural evolutionary process that applies to just about everything, including parks. Parks have to be maintained and updated so they serve the needs of visitors. There is no valid excuse to allow a park to deteriorate because of a concern about modifying a historical environment. Preserving shabbiness does not serve the public good. Those environments have to change and be updated. This type of challenge is posed in places with a long history such as Boston.

For example, a park must not be frozen in historical time. Boston Common is a prime example of that, being untouched by history and frozen in time—it needs new trees, new plantings, new benches, new paths, new lighting—it needs a complete makeover. It is also important to understand that monuments that are erected in parks are not central elements in experiencing a park. There is a geographic presence and the bringing together of man and the natural environment that outweighs the importance of any monuments that happen to be placed there. A monument highlights a historical event or a person and the monuments also may lose historical relevance. A park is used by the citizenry and has to be a dynamic and has to meet the needs of its users. So preservation of the historical character of a park should not be applied strictly, or else functionality will be lost. A park needs to evolve.

Boston Common is a great challenge because of its size. It wasn't designed as a park. It is a free-form piece of hilly real estate that nature created, and it is basically in its original state.

PRIDE IN HISTORICAL PRESERVATION

Thus, it is important to understand that just like a man-made park needs maintenance, so does a nature-made park. The problem from a preservation standpoint is this: the man-made park has original elements that can be reintroduced over and over again, like cookie dough is inserted into a cookie mold. So, for example, the annuals can be planted in the Public Garden every year. But with a nature-made park, there has to be intervention that will keep the park in good order. New plantings are necessary. Updating access paths and lighting is very important. In the case of the Common, that would go a long way to restore the pride in the area that is so important, especially in the light of the dark history of the place. It would be an act of redemption, which would be welcome to counter the negative history of the place.

BOSTON COMMON AND THE FIRST SNOW OF WINTER

Snow is a regular visitor during winter in New England. The question about snow is never if it will come, but rather when it will arrive. Snow can make its earliest appearance in November, but December sees the first significant amounts of snow. Then even larger amounts come in the first three months of the year. Winter weather in different parts of New England can vary significantly. The snowfall patterns and the character of the snow also varies. Boston Common being insulated by inland waters tends to to be shielded from winter's fury. The hardwood trees are spared by the mild winters. The first significant snowfall gives the Common a welcome and refreshing look. The tree branches take on a whitened appearance, making their outline much more distinct, and the grounds are covered with snow like frosting on a cake.

The pedestrian traffic through the park tends to decrease, as the cold and snow are major detractions. The park and the snow-covered surroundings serve as a barrier to easy movement through park space. Anyone who is familiar with the park has one or more shortcuts from one place to another. However, when the park is covered with snow, it is often not possible to use those shortcuts, and the trips tend to become longer and typically require much more effort. The park's role as a conduit between places—for example, from Beacon Hill to Downtown—is severely curtailed.

With an early light snow, the snow covering of the branches of the trees is the first snow to melt. Snow on the ground lingers, but not for long. Later in the winter season, the snow tends to remain when the temperature is very cold. The snow soon has a layer of ice over it, and it looks very different. In the sunlight, ice-covered snow glistens, while the softer, fluffy snow has a more matte appearance in the sun.

The first snowfall stirs up a feeling that I would call "the joy of snow." That feeling refers to the exhilaration people of all ages experience when the cold white visitor named snow comes. The experience is an example of the strong bond between man and nature in general and the love for snow that many people have. The adventurous among us want some direct involvement with snow, and before you know it, all sorts of snow inventions emerge—a snowman or a snow animal or an igloo—you name it, and it's mostly possible. When it comes to fashioning objects out of snow, there appears to be no limit to the imagination.

The prospect of moving on snow has great allure as well. People don cross country skis and use them to get about in areas that are impassable to traffic or in the park. And they would be happy to slide on sleds down any hill in sight. That attachment to snow makes it very popular when it comes at a leisurely pace and in moderate amounts. Animals, as well, seem to share that attachment to snow.

Snow in Boston Common can have varying appearances depending on the time of day and the outdoor temperature. Recently fallen snow often has a fluffy and powdery appearance. Melting snow has a slushy look and consistency. And snow exposed to very cold temperatures becomes icy. When trod upon, icy snow makes a creaky noise. Sunlight and artificial light are reflected in the snow. When the sun is strongest on a winter day, its direct light creates significant glare. Toward the end of the day, the snow briefly takes on the color of the setting sun, and at night with artificial lighting from streetlamps and the moon it reflects well, too.

BEACON HILL IN WINTER

The Beacon Hill community is the closest residential enclave to Boston Common. The low-lying part of the hill is Beacon Street, which abuts on the Common. The narrow hilly streets of Beacon Hill are difficult to access even when the weather is clear. The sidewalks are very narrow as well. They tend to require a strong walk on the upside. Access to automobiles is very limited under all circumstances and only a single lane is present on most streets. The problems with access to Beacon Hill are compounded many fold when the neighborhood is covered with snow. With heavy storms, shopping is sometimes possible on foot, but with great difficulty.

Also, let us say that you are undaunted by Beacon Hill. You are standing on the Beacon Street side of the Common, and you want to get to Cambridge Street. Before a snowstorm you could take Joy Street up the hill and then down the hill and get to Cambridge Street without difficulty. But after a snowstorm that route likely would be impassable.

Or let's say you wanted to get to a location on Mount Vernon Street, you could walk up Walnut Street but that, too, might not be possible after the storm. If you were in the Common and you needed to go to One Ashburton Place, generally you could easily walk past the State House to Bowdoin Street and walk up that street. But after a storm there is no guarantee that the option is available. So, people reroute their walking based on the size of the street and conditions in the street at the time.

The Beacon Hill neighborhood is of dwellings on a very steep hill. In its early history, when homes were built near the top of the hill, there was a chance to see the Charles River, or its estuary, which covered Back Bay and what is now the Public Garden. However, today that would be a great challenge; the buildings face the south and the north, and the river is mostly to the west, and there are many obstructions between the river and the buildings. The snow brings to Beacon Hill a certain tranquility that seems to say, "Slow down. It's time for quiet and contemplation." The otherwise vibrant community, like all others in the area, has to yield to nature's request.

STORMS AND STRESSES OF WINTER

Occasionally, there is a very large snowfall that blankets the area. Since people have a natural affinity to snow, there is a tendency to minimize the risks associated with a large snowstorm. Often people are unrealistic about their chances of getting caught in a storm, and they reason that it hadn't happened before, so why would it happen now? However, that reasoning is weak; it underestimates risk. A very heavy and rapid snowfall can come with little warning. When a blizzard comes, it can cause great damage, and bring people's daily activities to a halt.

Two years after the bicentennial, just such a storm descended on the area, with devastating effects. Dumping 27.1 inches of snow on the metropolitan area, the snowstorm at that time was one of the worst in the area's history. The Common and the rest of the city were under more than two feet of snow. For the Common, the consequences of such a severe snowstorm were relatively mild compared with those for the rest of the area. The trees, footpaths, park benches, and monuments were blanketed with snow, which had an effect on access and use of the park. But the park has no residents and no travelers in it, and it was mostly they who were most affected by the storm. For the rest of the city, the suburbs and the state and for the entire Northeast, the blizzard of 1978 brought immense damage and pain. The storm came on rather quickly and literally brought the area to its knees. It was like a knockout punch in a fight that was totally unforeseen. Within a few hours of the appearance of the storm, it disabled the highway system and, soon thereafter, it brought many of the daily and business activities of people to a screeching halt.

THE BLIZZARD OF 1978

A blizzard is defined as a very heavy snowstorm with the following features: high winds along with heavy accumulation of cold and driving dry snow. The definition is merely a functional one, which describes the basic elements of the severe snowstorm. However, the definition of a blizzard doesn't begin to address the human and environmental experience involved. Any person who has experienced a blizzard firsthand can testify to its immense power and potential for destruction. An early snowstorm blanketed the Northeast starting on January 20 and ending January 21. Approximately 21.4 inches of snow accumulated in Boston, placing the storm among the ten most severe snowstorms in Boston. But that storm was merely a prelude to a much more severe storm that would occur only two weeks later. That storm is referred to as the blizzard of 1978.

A blizzard in the Northeast occurs when certain weather conditions are met. First, there is a rainstorm that develops offshore, often in the lower mid-Atlantic coast. That storm carries warm and very moist air that tends to spread northward. The storm, a low pressure system, strengthens itself with moisture from the coastal waters. When it arrives in the area, it encounters a high pressure system with arctic air, and the blizzard develops when the storm brings high winds and snow.

On Sunday, February 5, 1978, a storm developed from an extratropical cyclone off the South Carolina coast. In New England at the time, there was an arctic cold front hovering over the area. The storm arrived in Massachusetts on the following day in the early afternoon and it intensified during the rush-hour period. It brought hurricane force winds of approximately 86 miles per hour. The typical snowstorm in the area lasts from six to twelve hours, but this storm lasted thirty-three hours, and when it was over, 27.1 inches of snow had fallen. The snow fell so rapidly that it brought traffic on the main interstate arteries to a halt. Drivers were stranded in their cars and pictures of Route 128 show a seemingly unending number of immobilized cars in the middle of a six-lane highway. The route looked like a parking lot. People who were stranded on the highways had to be rescued by snowmobiles. There were several fatalities owing to carbon monoxide exposure in cars with idling motors and exhaust pipes blocked by the snow. Over thirty-five hundred cars were found abandoned on the highways, mostly covered by snow.

At the time, the moon was full. The tides were high, and there was a storm surge, broken sea walls, and severe flooding. Trees were felled by the heavy storm, bringing down power lines and also causing damage to homes nearby. There were several fatalities related to contact with exposed electrical wiring in power lines that became disconnected in the storm.

With a natural event like a blizzard, it is difficult to predict its severity and the consequences it may have. There are so many variables involved. In the blizzard of 1978, it was both the intensity of the storm and the rapidity of its onset that was so devastating. One variable was a happenstance—the storm just developed one day before it arrived in Boston. It developed on a Sunday so it was not easy to inform people about it. Therefore, there was little notice and little time to prepare for the storm. Another important unforeseen variable was that the storm would arrive on the first business day of the week and at rush hour. That unfortunate timing was a major factor in some of the immediate damage it caused.

With storms, it is difficult to know exactly when and how hard they will hit. They are so often slowed en route. But we understand that paralysis of traffic on the highways in a snowstorm is a recipe for disaster. It doesn't take much for traffic to become snarled or brought to a standstill. Just a few cars have to be stopped in the lanes to block an entire highway. Motorists are very vulnerable to the effects of a severe weather disaster such as a blizzard. They mostly are not trained in self-extrication maneuvers, and they would not know how to best handle the situation. Extrication efforts by others are extremely difficult as access to marooned commuters in their cars is so limited. Also, the interstate highways have limited access, making them hazardous at times of natural disasters. Those highways were built to speed the flow of traffic and not with extrication issues in mind. Hence, it is an inescapable conclusion that those highways are a dangerous place in the time of a snowstorm, and the workday must be shortened when a storm is approaching. Highways should be closed at times of bad weather conditions, and the closing should occur before the storms arrival.

A WARMING TREND IN WINTER IS A PRELUDE TO SPRING

In the thick of winter, when the Common is frozen solid, there is a yearning for spring. Not long after the beginning of winter, the novelty of the season starts to wear off. The initial attraction to the season vanishes when the numbing cold becomes unrelenting and the white expanses of pristine snow change to ice or slush. People tire of the frigid weather and eagerly await a warming trend. People grow weary of cold ears, noses, necks, and hands, and wet and cold feet. They are quite prepared to banish the accoutrements of winter from the daily scene: sweaters, coats, hats, scarves, earmuffs, gloves, boots, rubbers, galoshes, and long underwear. Wishing for a less limiting pattern of weather, people look high and low for a thaw in winter. There is a silent yearning for a finale to the season, shared by people who work outdoors and suffer extremes of cold weather and those who love to be in the outdoors but are deterred by the cold. However, nature has its own mind, and we have to wait for it to decide when the time is right for a change in the weather pattern. And we all know that the time involved in waiting for any arrival is unpredictable.

Although spring officially comes in the third week of March, temperatures in Boston that month range from a low of 31 to a high of 46 degrees. So, March is still a rather cold month with significant snowfall, but generally less than in each of the preceding three months. Thus, a real thaw does not usually occur until April, which has an average temperature range of 41–56 degrees.

On the journey that is winter in Boston, the approach to spring may be compared to a voyage on a tranquil sea. On a given day, the weather may look good, but a storm may be developing at sea and may visit at any time with little warning. Spring officially begins on March 21, the date of the vernal equinox. The center of the earth is aligned with the center of the sun, which is directly overhead at the equator, and days and nights are of equal length in the Northern and Southern Hemispheres.

However, in New England, as in the Northeast in general, winter can linger way beyond that celestial event and snowstorms may come in April, and sometimes in early May as well. Thus, the end of winter and the beginning of spring do not necessarily coincide with the date of vernal equinox. Winter often extends from March into April, a period we can call "Indian winter." It seems ironic that the principal advantage of an extended summer, a longer hunting season, could be taken away by a delayed spring. But an advantage in nature is frequently nullified by a disadvantage. Moreover, man's plans for the seasons don't always coincide with nature's plans. But as the days move along in April, there is a warming trend, and early signs of spring appear, heralding the arrival of the new season, even if delayed.

In Boston Common, the early signs of spring the heavy rains of March, the return of the birds, and the reappearance of plant life. The early beginnings of plants appear after the long dormancy of winter. Leaf buds appear on the branches of trees before any of the early flowers sprout. Off the coast of Boston, about twenty-five miles to the north, the humpback whale returns from the Caribbean, and in the west the turkey vulture comes back. In people's backyards, wooden fences that have seen difficult days start to fall, it's time to service the car after trips to the mountains, and it's a perfect time for a spring cleanup. As winter draws to a close, and as the year draws to a close with it, Boston Common reaches a turning point at which a winter of mixed feelings will yield to a spring of hope. Thoughts of spring also bring the hope that the meaning in the events that occurred in the cycle of seasons over various one-hundred-year periods in our history will be revealed.

CENTENNIAL ANNIVERSARIES OF UNITED STATES INDEPENDENCE

A centennial, a period of one hundred years, is often considered in relation to the anniversary of a historical event or occasion. Many centennials commemorate events that happened on a single day. But the centennial of our independence, celebrated on July 4, the date that the Declaration of Independence was signed, is a celebration of the American Revolution, which lasted almost a decade (1775–1784). For the United States, there was no more important event in its history than the American Revolution, which freed us from the bondage of colonialism. That revolution changed the prospects of our country, opening up enormous opportunities. At the time, people could not foresee the immense changes that the American Revolution would bring to future generations. In many respects, the American Revolution may be compared to the exodus of the Israelites from Egypt as it was a signal historical event that shaped destiny. In the colonies, no matter how drastic was the abridgement of rights, no matter how encumbered was trade with tariffs and restrictions, no matter how bleak the prospects for the future, a significant number of people wished to remain loyal to England. Their loyalty was mostly to their British heritage, not to the colonial power.

In celebrating the centennial anniversary of an event, it is important to be mindful of the history before the event. That is because it is always important to understand how history unfolds. In doing so, we gain a larger perspective. Two centennials prior to the American Revolution—that is, in the year 1576—North America was in the hands of Native American peoples who mostly lived a nomadic existence, and in their hands, the land was mostly undeveloped. One centennial before, in 1676, about fifty to sixty years after the initial settlements, British immigrants were building their society and, in addition, commerce in the area was developing rapidly.

During the first hundred years after the country became independent from England, it developed rapidly in many spheres. The American Revolution, which liberated the colonists from the bonds of colonialism, was the principal catalyst of growth and development. It lifted the economic restrictions that inhibited growth during the colonial period. When that happened, the population grew rapidly, mostly from an increase in the birth rate of people who had settled in this country before the revolution but also from immigration from Europe. The country expanded toward the west by acquisition of land from foreign countries and from the migration of people to those lands in search of opportunity. The number of territories that became states increased as well. Toward the end of the first centennial, the country was ravaged by the Civil War, which caused much damage and pain to our nation and was a major setback in our development. The heavy burden of that conflict left the nation numbed and dispirited by the great loss of life and destruction of society from internecine warfare. However, the Industrial Revolution brought about rapid development in the United States during the last twenty-five years of the nineteenth century, which was the beginning of the next one hundred years. With the advent of the twentieth century, cities across the country developed rapidly, and the country became a world power.

There were major waves of immigration from Europe starting in the middle of the nineteenth century and extending into the last twenty-five years of the 1800s, and much of that immigration came initially through New York and spread to cities all over the country, including Boston. For immigrants, the United States was a country of the ultimate hope of freedom and prosperity. The immigrants came from areas where there was little hope, and they were attracted to the United States because of the prosperity the country enjoyed and the opportunities it offered. They participated in the building of the country and contributed in a very significant way to the industrial growth and development of the nation. During the twentieth century, the country was involved in two major world wars and an economic depression occurred in between after a decade of prosperity following the end of World War I. By the early 1940s, the country became the preeminent world power.

The development in Boston moved more slowly than in other places in the country following World War II. Downtown's skyline was quite empty until the decade before the bicentennial. You could say that one reason for that was the need for preservation of historical sites, which slowed the pace of development. However, that need was present later when the rate of development increased, so there had to be other reasons. You could say that from the perspective of business activities, each area has its own busy and quiet periods. But that really doesn't explain the actual phenomenon either. You could say the area was preoccupied and held back by other matters, and that is likely correct. But starting in 1970, with the bicentennial approaching, the gap between Boston and other cities started to close rapidly during a period of significant economic expansion, which featured a flourish of building activity in the city. In many ways, that period of growth put the area ahead of many others of comparable size. At the time, there was great optimism, and the feeling itself was enabling. As with most accomplishments of that magnitude, it takes a positive feeling to actually bring them about. There was strong determination with a willingness to take on new challenges. The net result was a surge in economic development, which came like a great wave splashing on the seashore with great force. The resulting economic boom brought hope to the area.

In the years approaching the bicentennial, there was much planning and preparation and a flurry of building activity. Completing important projects before the year of the bicentennial was a major goal, so that those projects would be included in the one-hundred-year period. The centennial is a celebration of an event in history with an examination of the accomplishments that have occurred during a specific time frame. So the preparation involves completing projects and accomplishing things before the period closes. Downtown, there were some large accomplishments that occurred in the ten years before the bicentennial. First, the city government moved from old city hall to new city hall. Second, Bank of Boston completed construction of its building at 100 Federal Street. Third, the Boston Federal Reserve built its new building next to the harbor and moved from its smaller building in Post Office

Square. We can say with confidence that only institutions with a keen sense of American history would want to complete large projects such as those before the bicentennial year, and they merit a special acknowledgment for that.

As the Common is liberated from winter's yoke, the somber mood created by this hilly preserve in that season changes gradually, and its overall disposition turns positive. With the approach of spring, we contemplate a thorough spring cleaning that will restore the natural beauty to the place. The broken branches will be removed and the lawns will be invigorated in the next season. The evil spirits in history conjured up in winter will be banished and replaced by a rebirth of hope in spring.

Boston Common has been a witness to history, having seen successive generations of inhabitants in the area from Native American times to the era starting with the English settlers. Each generation has many hopes for the next generation. Every family hopes that hardships suffered by the present and past generations will not be endured in the next or future generations. There is also the hope that the next generation will continue the work of the previous generation and will bring new accomplishments that will help the family prosper in the community and reach its goals. These are time-honored wishes in every family. But also to be considered are the collective hopes of society in an entire generation. One is that with the passing of time, society will become more advanced and creative, with new ideas, methods, and inventions leading to better living conditions. Education will be more prevalent and effective and rich in humanities and sciences, preparing people for the challenges they meet in daily life. Another hope is that there will be prosperity, with a balanced local economy that can provide broad opportunities for working people, including for those who recently completed their education. There is also hope that communication between countries will improve, and they will find ways to help themselves and one another, and trade will be conducted in free, equitable, and mutually beneficial patterns. Also, it is a fervent hope that any new challenges will be greeted with enthusiasm and met with resources and skills. Last, there is the wish that there will be growth and development and that the unfinished work of one generation will be continued in the next.

Under the best of circumstances, the generation of the present and the generations of the past will have unique identities. The generation of the present will face its own challenges, know its mind, prepare its agenda, and achieve its goals, and history will be a mere footnote to its accomplishments. We hope the successes of one generation will be surpassed by those of the next, and unfulfilled dreams of earlier generations will eventually be realized.

REFERENCES

BACK BAY HISTORY AND ARCHITECTURE

Aldrich, Megan. *Gothic Revival*. London, England: Phaidon Press Ltd., 1994.

Bunting, Bainbridge. *Houses of Boston's Back Bay: An Architectural History, 1840–1917.* Cambridge, Massachusetts: Belknap Press of Harvard University Press, 1967.

Clarke, Theodore G. *Beacon Hill, Back Bay, and the Building of Boston's Golden Age*. Charleston, South Carolina: History Press: 2010.

Hitchcock, Henry-Russell (1963). *Architecture: Nineteenth and Twentieth Centuries.* Penguin History of Art: Second Edition. New Haven, Connecticut: Yale University Press, 1963.

Martin, William. *Back Bay*. New York: Crown, 1979.

Moore, Barbara W., and Gail Weesner. *Back Bay: A Living Portrait*. Boston: Centry Hill Press, 1995.

Museum of Fine Arts Boston. *Back Bay Boston: The City as a Work of Art*. Boston, Massachusetts: Museum of Fine Arts, 1969.

Newman, William A., and Wilfred E. Holton. *Boston's Back Bay: The Story of America's Greatest Nineteenth-Century Landfill Project*. Boston, Massachusetts: Northeastern University Press, 2007.

O'Gorman, James F. *On the Boards: Drawings by Nineteenth-Century Boston Architects*. Philadelphia: University of Pennsylvania Press, 1989.

Sammarco, Anthony M. *Boston's Back Bay in the Victorian Era*. Portsmouth, New Hampshire: Arcadia, 2003.

Shand-Tucci, Douglas. *Built in Boston: City and Suburb, 1800–2000*. Amherst, Massachusetts: The University of Massachusetts Press, 1999.

Southworth, Susan, and Michael Southworth. *AIA Guide to Boston*. 3rd edition. Guilford, Connecticut: Globe Pequot Press, 2008.

COMMONWEALTH AVENUE
Commonwealth Avenue in Process, 1872. Graphic, 1872.

Fuller and Whitney Boston. Sectional Plans of Commonwealth Avenue Lands from Dartmouth Street to West Chester Park. Boston: 1882.

Norton, Bettina A. *Neighborhood Trivia Hunt for Boston's Back Bay*. Boston, Massachusetts: Ban Publishing Company, 1985.

Sargent, Charles S. *The Trees of Commonwealth Avenue, Boston*. Brookline, Massachusetts: Printed for the Author, 1909.

BOSTON VENDOME HOTEL AND ITS LIGHTING CONSULTANT, THOMAS A. EDISON

Baldwin, Neil. *Edison: Inventing the Century*. Chicago: University of Chicago Press, 2001.

Burns, Elmer E. *The Story of Great Inventions*. New York and London: Harper & Brothers, 1910.

Clark, Ronald W. *Edison: The Man Who Made the Future*. London: Macdonald & Jane's, 1977.

Conot, Robert. *A Streak of Luck*. New York: Seaview Books, 1979.

Davis, L. J. *Fleet Fire: Thomas Edison and the Pioneers of the Electric Revolution*. New York: Arcade Pub., 2003.

Edison, Thomas A. *Menlo Park: The Early Years, April 1876–December 1877*. Edited by Rosenberg, Robert A., Paul B. Israel, Keith A. Nier, and Melodie Andrews. Baltimore, Maryland: Johns Hopkins University Press, 1989.

Evans, Harold. *They Made America*. New York: Little, Brown and Company, 2004.

Homans, James E., ed. "Edison, Thomas Alva." *The Cyclopædia of American Biography*. New York: The Press Association Compilers, Inc., 1918.

Israel, Paul B. *Edison: A Life of Invention*. New York: John Wiley & Sons, 2000.

Jenkins, Reese V., ed. *The Papers of Thomas A. Edison.* Baltimore, Maryland: Johns Hopkins University Press, 1989.

Josephson, Matthew. *Edison: A Biography.* New York: McGraw Hill, 1959.

King, Moses. *The Back-Bay District and the Vendome.* Boston: M. King, 1880.

Klein, Maury. *The Power Makers: Steam, Electricity, and the Men Who Invented Modern America.* New York: Bloomsbury Publishing, 2008.

Shulman, Seth. *Owning the Future.* Boston: Houghton Mifflin Company, 1999.

Stross, Randall E. *The Wizard of Menlo Park: How Thomas Alva Edison Invented the Modern World.* New York: Crown Publishers, 2007.

BOYLSTON STREET

Boylston Family Papers: 1688–1979. Massachusetts Historical Society. Call Number: Ms. N-4.

Drake, Samuel A. *Old Landmarks and Historic Personages of Boston.* Boston: James R. Osgood and Co., 1873.

Johnson, Frederick, and Henry C. Stetson. *The Boylston Street Fishweir, a Study of the Archaeology, Biology, and Geology of a Site on Boylston Street in the Back Bay District of Boston, Massachusetts.* Andover, Massachusetts: Phillips Academy, the Foundation, 1942.

COPLEY SQUARE AND VICINITY

Barratt, Carrie R.; Metropolitan Museum of Art. *John Singleton Copley in America*. New York: The Metropolitan Museum of Art, 1995. Distributed by H. N. Abrams.

Prown, Jules D. *John Singleton Copley in America, 1738–1774*. Cambridge, Massachusetts: Published for the National Gallery of Art, Washington, by Harvard University Press, 1966.

Rocheleau, Matt. Back Bay T Station Roof to Be Replaced. *Boston Globe* (September 21, 2010): B.5.

OLD SOUTH CHURCH

Hill, Hamilton A., and A. P. C. Griffin. *History of the Old South Church (Third Church) Boston, 1669–1884*. Boston and New York: Houghton, Mifflin and Company, 1890.

History of the Old South Church of Boston. Published for the benefit of the Old South Fund, 1890.

THE THREE JOHN HANCOCK BUILDINGS

Botwright, Ken O. "Hancock's Ugly Duckling Plans April '75 Plywood Sale." *Boston Globe* (September 1, 1974): 1.

Cambell, Robert. "A Blue Mirage; the John Hancock Tower Shimmers in the Sun, Mirroring the Old and New; in Boston, Aloof and Cool. It's a Star of the City's architecture; Both Loved and Hated." *Boston Globe Magazine* (May 31, 1981): 1.

Cobb, Nathan. "The Panes of Big John." *Boston Globe* (April 22, 1973): C4.

Cobb, Nathan. "Hancock Tower to Test 18 Thicker Glass Panes. *Boston Globe* (June 10, 1973): 50.

Curwood, Stephen. "Hancock Sues over Tower Glass." *Boston Globe* (September 16, 1975): 1.

Cushing, George M., and Ross Urquhart. *Great Buildings of Boston: A Photographic Guide.* New York, New York: Dover Publications, 1982.

Hammond, James. "Hancock Tower Officially Open." *Boston Globe* (September 30, 1976): A.8.

Langner, Paul. "Glass Returns to Hancock Tower." *Boston Globe* (July 28, 1973): 28.

"Latest Count on Hancock Windows." *Boston Globe* (December 31, 1978): 3.

Morgan, Keith, and Naomi Miller. "Buildings of Massachusetts: Metropolitan Boston." In *Buildings of the United States.* Charlottesville, Virginia: University of Virginia Press, 2009.

"Now the New Hancock Tower Needs Reinforcing. *Boston Globe* (March 20, 1975): 3.

Pave, Marvin. "City May Order John Hancock Tower Vacated." *Boston Globe* (March 21, 1976): 3.

Puleo, Stephen. *A City So Grand: The Rise of an American Metropolis, Boston 1850–1900*. Boston: Beacon Press, 2011.

Yudis, Anthony. "John Hancock Unveils 60-Story 'Mirror.'" *Boston Globe* (November 28, 1967): 1.

Yudis, Anthony. "Hancock, City Agree On Tower." *Boston Globe* (February 1, 1968): 1.

BOSTON PUBLIC GARDEN

Barker, George. "Stereographs of Boston and Cambridge, Massachusetts" [graphic]. Niagara Falls, New York: Geo. Barker, 1889.

Boston (Mass.) Committee on the Public Lands., and Samuel Gardner Drake Pamphlet Collection (Library of Congress). *Report of the Joint Committee on Public Lands in Relation to the Public Garden, July 1850*. Boston: J. H. Eastburn, City Printer, 1850.

"Boston Public Garden, as It Should Be." *Gleason's Pictorial*. Boston: Forgotten Books, 1853.

Davenport, Arthur. "Boston's Uncommon Park." *New York Times* (September 27, 1964): Page xxii.

Heath, Edwin G. "From Round Marsh to Public Garden." *The Bostonian* 2, 6 (1895)Highsmith, Carol M. "Iconic Swan Boat Awaits Passengers at the Lagoon, the Boston Public Garden, Boston, Massachusetts" [graphic]. Carol M. Highsmith Archive, 1980.

Highsmith, Carol M. "Idyllic Lagoon in the Public Garden, Created in 1837, Boston, Massachusetts" [graphic]. Carol M. Highsmith Archive, 1980.

Keystone View Company. "Scene in Public Gardens, Boston, Massachusetts" [graphic]. Meadville, Pennsylvania: Keystone View Company, 1929.

Lee, Henry., and Friends of the Public Garden and Common. *The Public Garden, Boston*. Boston: Friends of the Public Garden and Common, 1988.

McCloskey, Robert. *Make Way for Ducklings*. New York: The Viking Press, 1941.

Public Garden Map and Notable Trees. City of Boston Website. Boston. gov/park/public-garden.

Prendergast, Maurice. *Large Boston Public Garden Sketchbook*. 1st edition. New York: G. Braziller, in association with the Metropolitan Museum of Art, 1987.

Slack, Donovan. "Thou Art No Romeo." *Boston Globe* (August 12, 2005): A.1.

Stevens, Charles W. "Boston Public Garden." *The New England Magazine* Boston: Warren F Kellogg: Volume XXIV pp.343–356. March-August, 1901.

Wright, Horace W. *Birds of the Boston Public Garden: A Study in Migration*. Cambridge, Massachusetts: Houghton Mifflin Co., Riverside Press, 1909.

BOSTON COMMON

Adams, Nehemiah, William D. Ticknor, and Henry B. Williams. *Boston Common*. Boston: W. D. Ticknor and H. B. Williams, 1842.

Albree, John. *A Blight on Boston: How Shall It Be removed?* Boston: Berkeley Press, 1906.

Ayer, Mary F. *Boston Common in Colonial and Provincial Days*. Boston: Private Printing, 1903.

Ayer, Mary F., and D. B. Updike; Merrymount Press. *Early Days on Boston Common*. Boston: Private Printing, 1910.

Barber, Samuel. *Boston Common*. Boston: Christopher Publishing House, 1914.

Barber, Samuel. *Boston Common: A Diary of Notable Events, Incidents, and Neighboring Occurrences*. Boston: Christopher Publishing House, 1916.

Barker, George. "Stereographs of Boston and Cambridge, Massachusetts" [graphic]. Niagara Falls, New York: Geo. Barker, 1889.

Boston Industrial School for Crippled and Deformed Children. *Boston Common in the Seventeenth Century*. Boston: Industrial School for Crippled and Deformed Children, 1903.

Boston (Mass.) Committee of Citizens., and William H. Whitmore. *The Public Rights in Boston Common. Being the Report of a Committee of Citizens*. Boston: Press of Rockwell and Churchill, 1877.

Curtis, Joseph H. *Life of Campestris Ulm, the Oldest Inhabitant of Boston Common*. Boston: W. B. Clarke, 1910.

Farber, Norman, and Arnold Lobel. *As I Was Crossing Boston Common*. New York: E. P. Dutton, 1975.

Friends of the Public Garden and Common. *Boston Common*. Charleston, South Carolina: Acadia, 2005.

Goodspeed, C. E. "Park Square in 1837 from a Rare Contemporary Lithograph." Graphic. Boston: Published by Charles E. Goodspeed, 5A Park St., 1902.

Highsmith, Carol. M. (1980). "Boston Common, Boston, Massachusetts" [graphic]. Carol M. Highsmith Archive, 1980.

Howe, M. A. De Wolfe. *Boston Common: Scenes from Four Centuries*. Boston and New York: Houghton Mifflin Company, 1921.

Kahn, Ric. "Crackdown on the Common: Activist Complains Homeless Targeted." *Boston Globe* (June 23, 1995): 21.

Karlsen, Carol F. *The Devil in the Shape of a Woman: Witchcraft in Colonial New England*. New York: Norton, 1998.

Story of the Old Elm on Boston Common. Boston: Press of J. Wilson, 1876.

McNulty, Elizabeth. *Boston Then and Now*. San Diego, California: Thunder Bay Press, 1999.

Thomas, Jack. "Boston Common's Bloody Past." *Boston Globe,* (July 2, 1995): 59

"Tremont St., Boston, Mass." [graphic]. U.S. Geog. File, 1901.

Warren, J. C. *The Great Tree on Boston Common*. Boston: John Wilson & Son, 1855.

Yang, John. "Mayor Foils Purse-Snatcher's Escape." *Boston Globe* (December 13, 1980): 1.

PARK SQUARE

Esposito, John C. *Fire in the Grove: The Cocoanut Grove Tragedy and Its Aftermath*. Cambridge, Massachusetts: Da Capo Press, 2005.

"Flame Proofing Assailed." *Daily Boston Globe* (December 11, 1942): 1, 18.

"Grove Seated over 1,000; One of the Largest Night Clubs." *Daily Boston Globe* (November 29, 1942): A.29.

Keyes, Edward. *Cocoanut Grove*. New York: Atheneum, 1984.

Saffle J. R. "The 1942 Fire at Boston's Cocoanut Grove Nightclub." *Am J Surg* 166, 6 (1993): 581–91.

Schorow, Stephanie. *Boston on Fire: A History of Fires and Firefighting in Boston*. Beverly, Massachusetts: Commonwealth Editions, 2003.

Schorow, Stephanie. *The Cocoanut Grove Fire*. Beverly, Massachusetts, Commonwealth Editions, 2005.

BEACON HILL

Alcott, Louisa M. *Jack and Jill, a Village Story.* Boston: Little, Brown, and Company, 1928.

Alcott, Louisa M. *Jo's Boys and How They Turned Out: A Sequel to* Little Men. Boston: Little, Brown, and Company, 1925.

Alcott, Louisa M. *Little Men: Life at Plumfield with Jo's Boys.* Boston: Little, Brown, and Company, 1924.

Alcott, Louisa. M. *An Old-Fashioned Girl.* Boston: Little, Brown, and Company, 1926.

Alcott, Louisa M. *Rose in Bloom: A Sequel to* Eight Cousins. Boston: Little, Brown, and Company, 1927.

Alcott, Louisa M.*Under the Lilacs.* Boston, Massachusetts: Little, Brown, and Company,1928.

"Area Preservation and the Beacon Hill Bill." *Old-Time New England* 46 (164) (Spring 1956)

Green, Martin B. *The Mount Vernon Street Warrens: A Boston Story, 1860–1910.* New York: Charles Scribner's Sons, 1989.

Keyes, Frances P. *Joy Street.* New York: Messner, 1950.

McIntyre, A. McVoy. *Beacon Hill: A Walking Tour.* Boston: Little, Brown, and Company, 1975.

Moying, Li-Marcus. *Beacon Hill: The Life and Times of a Neighborhood.* Boston: Northeastern University Press, 2002.

Stapp, Emile B., and Jeannette A. Stewart. *The Little Streets of Beacon Hill.* Cambridge, Massachusetts: J. F. Olsson and Company, 1928.

HISTORY OF BOSTON AND MASSACHUSETTS BAY COLONY

PRECOLONIAL TIMES: INDIANS OF THE ALGONQUIAN NATION

Brownstone, David M., and Irene M. Franck. *Historic Places of Early America.* New York: Aladdin Books, 1989.

Carpenter, Roger M. *"Times Are Altered with Us": American Indians from Contact to the New Republic.* Chichester, West Sussex, United Kingdom: John Wiley & Sons Inc., 2014.

Morgan, Philip D., and Molly A. Warsh. *Early North America in Global Perspective.* New York: Routledge/Taylor & Francis Group, 2014.

Richter, Daniel K. *Before the Revolution: America's Ancient Pasts.* Cambridge, Massachusetts: Belknap Press of Harvard University Press, 2011.

EARLY COLONIAL TIMES (1620–1760): PILGRIMS

Abrams, Ann U. *The Pilgrims and Pocahontas: Rival Myths of American Origin.* Boulder, Colorado: Westview Press, 1999.

Doherty, Kieran. *William Bradford: Rock of Plymouth*. Brookfield, Connecticut: Twenty-First Century Books, 1999.

Goodwin, John A. *The Pilgrim Republic: An Historical Review of the Colony of New Plymouth*. Boston: Houghton Mifflin Co., 1920 [1879].

Gould, Philip. "William Bradford 1590–1657." In Lauter, Paul. *The Heath Anthology of American Literature: Beginnings to 1800*. Boston: Houghton Mifflin, 2009.

Haxtun, Annie A. *Signers of the Mayflower Compact*. Baltimore, Maryland: The Mail and Express, 1899.

Moe, Barbara A. *The Charter of the Massachusetts Bay Colony: A Primary Source Investigation of the 1629 Charter*. 1st edition. New York: Rosen Primary Source, 2003.

Philbrick, Nathaniel. *Mayflower: A Story of Community, Courage and War*. New York: Penguin Books, 2006.

Sargent, Mark L. "William Bradford's 'Dialogue' with History." *The New England Quarterly* 65, 3 (1992): 389–421.

Schmidt, Gary D. *William Bradford: Plymouth's Faithful Pilgrim*. Grand Rapids, Michigan: William B. Eerdmans Publishing Co., 1999.

Stratton, Eugene A. *Plymouth Colony: Its History & People, 1620–1691* Lehi, Utah: Ancestry Incorporated, 1986.

Wenska, Walter P. "Bradford's Two Histories: Pattern and Paradigm in 'Of Plymouth Plantation.'" *Early American Literature* 13, 2 (Fall 1978): 151–164.

William Bradford Correspondence, 1638–1648. Manuscript Division, The Library of Congress, Washington D.C..

WILLIAM BLAXTON, FIRST ENGLISH SETTLER ON THE SHAWMUT PENINSULA

Amory, Thomas C. *William Blackstone, Boston's First Inhabitant.* 2nd edition. Boston: Rockwell & Churchill, 1877.

DeCosta, B. F. *William Blackstone in His Relation to Massachusetts and Rhode Island.* New York: Mallory, 1880.

Lind, Louise. *William Blackstone, Sage of the Wilderness.* Bowie, Maryland: Heritage Books, 1993.

PURITANS

Bolte, Marie, and Dante Ginevra. *Arrested for Witchcraft!: Nickolas Flux and the Salem Witch Trials.* North Mankato, Minnesota: Capstone Press, 2014.

Bremer, Francis J. *Lay Empowerment and the Development of Puritanism.* New York: Palgrave Macmillan, 2015.

Carpenter, John B. "New England's Puritan Century: Three Generations of Continuity in the City upon a Hill." *Fides Et Historia* 30 (2003): 1.

Clark, Beth. *Anne Hutchinson: Religious Leader.* Philadelphia: Chelsea House Publishers, 2000.

Coffey, John, and Paul C. H. Lim. *The Cambridge Companion to Puritanism*. Cambridge, England: Cambridge University Press, 2008.

Collier, Christopher, and James L Collier. *Pilgrims and Puritans, 1620–1676*. New York: Benchmark Books, 1998.

Collins, Owen. *Speeches That Changed the World*. Louisville, Kentucky: Westminster John Knox Press, 1999.

Gardiner, Samuel R. *The First Two Stuarts and the Puritan Revolution*. New York: C. Scribner's Sons, 1895.

Faber, Doris, and Frank Vaughn. *A Colony Leader: Anne Hutchinson*. Champaign, Illinois: Garrard Publishing Company, 1970.

Giussani, Luigi. *American Protestant Theology: A Historical Sketch*. Montreal, Quebec; Kingston, Ontario: McGill-Queen's University Press, 2013.

Kent, Deborah. *Witchcraft Trials: Fear, Betrayal, and Death in Salem*. Berkeley Heights, New Jersey: Enslow Publishers, 2009.

Lancelott, Francis. *The Queens of England and Their Times*. New York: D. Appleton and Co., 1858

Lewis, C. S., and Walter Hooper. *Selected Literary Essays*. London: Cambridge University Press, 1969.

Morone, James A. *Hellfire Nation: The Politics of Sin in American History*. New Haven, Connecticut: Yale University Press, 2003.

Morris, M. Michelle Jarrett. *Under Household Government: Sex and Family in Puritan Massachusetts.* Cambridge, Massachusetts: Harvard University Press, 2013.

Neal, Daniel. *The History of the Puritans.* New York: Harper, 1844.

Neuman, Meredith M. *Jeremiah's Scribes: Creating Sermon Literature in Puritan New England.* Philadelphia: University of Pennsylvania Press, 2013.

Pell, Ed. *John Winthrop: Governor of the Massachusetts Bay Colony.* Mankato, Minnesota: Capstone Press, 2004.

Spurr, John. *English Puritanism, 1603–1689.* New York: Saint Martin's Press, 1998.

West, Jim. *Drinking with Calvin and Luther!* Lincoln, California: Oakdown Books, 2003.

Winthrop, John. *John Winthrop Papers.* circa 1630. Manuscript Division, Library of Congress, Washington, D.C.

LIFE IN COLONIAL AMERICA

Dosier, Susan. *Colonial Cooking.* North Mankato, Minnesota: Capstone Press, 2017.

Irwin, Raymond D. *Books on Early American History and Culture, 1996–2000: An Annotated Bibliography.* Santa Barbara, California: Praeger, 2011.

Hakim, Joy. *From Colonies to Country*. New York: Oxford University Press, 1993.

Johnson, Claudia D. *Daily Life in Colonial New England*. Westport, Connecticut: Greenwood Press, 2002.

King, David C., and Bobbie Moore. *Colonial Days: Discover the Past with Fun Projects, Games, Activities, and Recipes*. New York: J. Wiley & Sons, 1998.

Nichols, Joan K., and Dan Krovatin. *A Matter of Conscience: The Trial of Anne Hutchinson*. Austin, Texas: Raintree Steck-Vaughn, 1993.

Rowse, A. L. "New England in the Earliest Days." *American Heritage* 10, 5 (August 1959): 22.

Sabin, Louis, and Hal Frenck. *Colonial Life in America*. Mahwah, New Jersey: Troll Associates, 1985.

Schultz, Eric B., and Mike Tougias. *King Philip's War: The History and Legacy of America's Forgotten Conflict*. 1st edition. Woodstock, Vermont: Countryman Press, 1999.

Sheppard, Ruth. *Empires Collide: The French and Indian War 1754–63*. Oxford and New York: Osprey, 2006.

Winters, Kay, and Larry Day. *Colonial Voices: Hear Them Speak*. 1st edition. New York: Dutton Children's Books, 2008.

Wolfe, James, and Barbara A. Moe. *Understanding the Charter of the Massachusetts Bay Colony*. New York: Enslow Publishing, 2016.

BOSTON FROM 1765 TO 1775: A CAULDRON OF DISCONTENT IN THE PRELUDE TO THE AMERICAN REVOLUTION

Archer, Richard. *As If an Enemy's Country: The British Occupation of Boston and the Origins of Revolution.* Oxford and New York: Oxford University Press, 2010.

Deming, Brian. *Boston and the Dawn of American Independence.* Yardley, Pennsylvania: Westholme, 2013.

Maier, Pauline. *From Resistance to Revolution: Colonial Radicals and the Development of American Opposition to Britain, 1765–1776.* New York: Knopf, 1972.

Sutton, Felix, and Bill Barss. *Sons of Liberty.* New York: J. Messner, 1969.

BOSTON PATRIOTS

SAMUEL ADAMS, POLITICIAN

Adams, Samuel and Harry A. Cushing, eds. *The Writings of Samuel Adams.* 4 volumes. New York: G. P. Putnam's Sons, 1904–08.

Alexander, John. *Samuel Adams: America's Revolutionary Politician.* Lanham, Maryland: Rowman and Littlefield, 2002.

Becker, Carl L. "Samuel Adams." *Dictionary of American Biography, Volume 1*: 95–101. New York, New York: Scribner's, 1928.

Burgan, Michael. *Samuel Adams: Patriot and Statesman.* Minneapolis, Minnesota: Compass Point Books, 2005.

Davis, Kate. *Samuel Adams*. San Diego, California: Blackbirch Press, 2002.

Farley, Karin C. *Samuel Adams: Grandfather of His Country*. Austin, Texas: Raintree Steck-Vaughn, 1995.

Fowler, William M., Jr. *Samuel Adams: Radical Puritan*. New York: Longman, 1997.

Fritz, Jean, and Trina S. Hyman. *Why Don't You Get a Horse, Sam Adams?* New York: Coward, McCann & Geoghegan, 1974.

Hosmer, James K. *Samuel Adams*. Boston: Houghton Mifflin, 1885.

Maier, Pauline. "Coming to Terms with Samuel Adams." *American Historical Review* 81, 1 (1976): 12–37.

Maier, Pauline *The Old Revolutionaries: Political Lives in the Age of Samuel Adams*. New York: Knopf, 1980.

Maier, Pauline "Samuel Adams." In John A. Garraty and Mark C. Carnes, eds., *American National Biography*. New York: Oxford University Press, 1999.

Miller, John C. *Sam Adams: Pioneer in Propaganda*. Boston: Little, Brown, 1936.

Nobles, Gregory. "Yet the Old Republicans Still Persevere: Samuel Adams, John Hancock, and the Crisis of Popular Leadership in Revolutionary Massachusetts, 1775–90." In Ronald Hoffman and Peter J. Albert, eds., *The Transforming Hand of Revolution: Reconsidering the American Revolution as a Social Movement*, 258–85. Charlottesville, Virginia: University Press of Virginia, 1995.

O'Toole, James M. "The Historical Interpretations of Samuel Adams." *New England Quarterly* 49 (March 1976): 82–96.

Puls, Mark. *Samuel Adams: Father of the American Revolution*. New York: Palgrave Macmillan, 2006.

Raphael, Ray. *Founding Myths: Stories That Hide Our Patriotic Past*. New York: The New Press, 2004.

Stoll, Ira. *Samuel Adams: A Life*. New York: Free Press, 2008.

Thomas, Peter D. G. *The Townshend Duties Crisis: The Second Phase of the American Revolution, 1767–1773*. Oxford and New York: Oxford University Press, 1987.

Wells, William V. *The Life and Public Services of Samuel Adams: Being a Narrative of His Acts and Opinions, and of His Agency in Producing and Forwarding the American Revolution, with Extracts from His Correspondence, State Papers, and Political Essays*. 3 volumes. Boston: Little, Brown, 1865.

JOHN HANCOCK, MERCHANT

Allan, Herbert S. *John Hancock: Patriot in Purple*. New York: Macmillan, 1948.

Baxter, William T. *The House of Hancock: Business in Boston, 1724–1775*. Cambridge, Massachusetts: Harvard University Press, 1945.

Brandes, Paul D. *John Hancock's Life and Speeches: A Personalized Vision of the American Revolution, 1763–1793*. Lanham, Maryland: Scarecrow Press, 1996.

Brown, Richard D. *Revolutionary Politics in Massachusetts: The Boston Committee of Correspondence and the Towns, 1772–1774*. Cambridge, Massachusetts: Harvard University Press, 1970.

Fowler, William M., Jr. *The Baron of Beacon Hill: A Biography of John Hancock*. Boston: Houghton Mifflin, 1980.

Hancock, John, and Abram E. Brown. *John Hancock, His book*. Boston: 1898.

Proctor, Donald J. "John Hancock: New Soundings on an Old Barrel." *The Journal of American History* 64, 3 (December 1977): 652–77.

Reid, John P. *In a Rebellious Spirit: The Argument of Facts, the Liberty Riot, and the Coming of the American Revolution*. University Park, Pennsylvania: Pennsylvania State University Press, 1979.

Sears, Lorenzo. *John Hancock, The Picturesque Patriot*. Boston: Gregg Press, 1972.

Tyler, John W. *Smugglers and Patriots: Boston Merchants and the Advent of the American Revolution*. Boston: Northeastern University Press, 1986.

Unger, Harlow G. *John Hancock: Merchant King and American Patriot*. New York: Wiley & Sons, 2000.

Wolkins, George G. "The Seizure of John Hancock's Sloop *Liberty*." *Proceedings of the Massachusetts Historical Society* 55 (1923): 239–84.

JOSEPH WARREN, PHYSICIAN

Cary, John. *Joseph Warren: Physician, Politician, Patriot*. Chicago: University of Illinois Press, 1961.

Frothingham, Richard. *Life and Times of Joseph Warren*. Boston: Little, Brown, & Company, 1865.

Hardman, Ron, and Jessica Hardman. *Shadow Fox: Sons of Liberty*. Fox Run Press, 2010.

Wilson, James G., and John Fiske, eds. *Appleton's Cyclopedia of American Biography*. 6 volumes. New York: D. Appleton and Company, 1887–89.

PAUL REVERE, SILVERSMITH

Brooks, Victor. *The Boston Campaign: April 1775–March 1776*. Conshohocken, Pennsylvania: Combined Publishing, 1999.

Drake, Samuel A. *Historic Mansions and Highways around Boston*. Boston: Little, Brown, 1899.

Falino, Jeannine, J., Gerald W. R. Ward, Museum of Fine Arts, Boston, and Colonial Society of Massachusetts. *New England Silver and Silversmithing: 1620–1815*. Charlottesville, Virginia: University Press of Virginia, 2001.

Federhen, Deborah. *From Artisan to Entrepreneur: Paul Revere's Silver Shop Operation*. Boston: Paul Revere Memorial Association, 1988.

Fischer, David H. *Paul Revere's Ride.* New York: Oxford University Press, 1994.

Forbes, Esther. *Paul Revere and the World He Lived In.* Boston: Houghton Mifflin Company, 1942.

Gettemy, Charles. *The True Story of Paul Revere.* Boston: Little, Brown, 1905.

Goss, Elbridge H. *The Life of Colonel Paul Revere.* Boston: J. G. Cupples, 1891.

Longfellow, Henry W. "Paul Revere's Ride." *Atlantic Monthly* 7, 39 (1861): 27.

Martello, Robert. *Midnight Ride, Industrial Dawn: Paul Revere and the Growth of American Enterprise. Johns Hopkins Studies in the History of Technology.* Baltimore, Maryland: The Johns Hopkins University Press, 2010.

McDonald, Forrest, and Ellen McDonald. "The Ethnic Origins of the American People, 1790." *The William and Mary Quarterly.* 37, 2 (April 1980): 179–199.

Miller, Joel J. *The Revolutionary Paul Revere.* Nashville, Tennessee: Thomas Nelson, 2010.

Murrin, John M.; et al. *Liberty, Equality, Power: A History of the American People. Volume I: to 1877.* Florence, Kentucky: Wadsworth-Thomson Learning, 2002 [1996].

Paul Revere, Artisan, Businessman and Patriot: The Man behind the Myth. Boston: Paul Revere Memorial Association, 1988.

Revere, Paul. *Paul Revere's Three Accounts of His Famous Ride.* Introduction by Morgan, Edmund. Boston: Massachusetts Historical Society, 1961.

Steblecki, Edith J. *Paul Revere and Freemasonry.* Boston: Paul Revere Memorial Association, 1985.

Triber, Jayne. *A True Republican: The Life of Paul Revere.* Amherst, Massachusetts: University of Massachusetts Press, 1998.

BRITISH COLONIAL ADMINISTRATORS

FRANCIS BERNARD, GOVERNOR OF MASSACHUSETTS BAY COLONY

Anderson, Fred. *Crucible of War: The Seven Years' War and the Fate of Empire in British North America, 1754–1766.* New York: Alfred Knopf, 2000.

Barrington, Viscount William W., and Sir Francis Bernard. *The Barrington-Bernard Correspondence and Illustrative Matter, 1760–1770.* Cambridge, Massachusetts: Harvard University Press, 1912.

Burke, Sir Bernard, and Ashworth P. Burke. *General and Heraldic Dictionary of the Peerage and Baronetage.* London: Burke's Peerage Limited, 1914.

Dowd, Gregory Evans. *War under Heaven: Pontiac, the Indian Nations, & the British Empire.* Baltimore, Maryland: Johns Hopkins University Press, 2002.

Galvin, John. *Three Men of Boston.* New York: Thomas Y. Crowell, 1976.

Higgins, Sophia. *The Bernards of Abington and Nether Winchendon: A Family History.* London and New York: Longmans, Green, 1903.

Lurie, Maxine, ed. *Encyclopedia of New Jersey.* New Brunswick, New Jersey: Rutgers University Press, 2004.

Nason, Elias, and George Varney. *A Gazetteer of the State of Massachusetts.* Boston: B. B. Russell, 1890.

Nicolson, Colin. "Governor Francis Bernard, the Massachusetts Friends of Government, and the Advent of the Revolution." Proceedings of the Massachusetts Historical Society, Third Series, Volume 103 (1991): 24–113.

Nicolson, Colin. *The "Infamas Govener" Francis Bernard and the Origins of the American Revolution.* Boston: Northeastern University Press, 2000.

Shy, John. *A People Numerous and Armed: Reflections on the Military Struggle for American independence.* Ann Arbor, Michigan: University of Michigan Press, 1990.

Walett, Francis. "Governor Bernard's Undoing: An Earlier Hutchinson Letters Affair." *The New England Quarterly* 38, 2 (June 1965): 217–26.

THOMAS GAGE, GENERAL AND GOVERNOR OF MASSACHUSETTS BAY COLONY

Alden, John R. *General Gage in America: Being Principally a History of His Role in the American Revolution*. Baton Rouge, Louisiana: Louisiana State University Press, 1948.

Hinman, Bonnie. *Thomas Gage: British General*. Philadelphia: Chelsea House, 2002.

Stephen, Leslie, ed. "Gage, Thomas (1721–1787)." *Dictionary of National Biography*. Volume 20. London: Smith, Elder & Co., 1889.

BRITISH MILITARY OFFICERS

JOHN BURGOYNE, GENERAL

Billias, George A. *George Washington's Opponents*. New York: William Morrow, 1969.

Huddleston, F. J. *Gentleman Johnny Burgoyne, Misadventures of an English General in the Revolution*. New York: Bobbs-Merrill Company, Garden City Publishers, 1927.

Humphreys, Chris C. *Jack Absolute, The Blooding of Jack Absolute, Absolute Honour*. New York: Thomas Dunne Books/St. Martin's Press, 2004.

Mintz, Max M. *The Generals of Saratoga: John Burgoyne & Horatio Gates:* New Haven, Connecticut: Yale University Press, 1990.

Shaw, George B. *The Devil's Disciple*. London: Dent, 1966.

Stephens, Henry M. "Burgoyne, John (1722–1792)." *Dictionary of National Biography.* London: Smith, Elder & Co, 1885–1900.

Stokesbury, James. "Burgoyne Biography." *Dictionary of Canadian Biography vol. 4 (1771-1800) University of Toronto, Universite Laval, Archives of Canada 1979-2011.*

Thomson, Peter. *The Cambridge Introduction to English Theatre, 1660–1900.* Cambridge: Cambridge University Press, 2006.

Watt, Gavin K. *The British Campaign of 1777, Volume Two: The Burgoyne Expedition: Burgoyne's native and loyalist auxiliaries*, Milton, Ontario: Global Heritage Press, 2013.

HENRY CLINTON, GENERAL

Clement, R. "The World Turned Upside Down at the Surrender of Yorktown." *Journal of American Folklore* 92, 363 (January–March 1979): 66–67.

Ferling, John. *The World Turned Upside Down: The American Victory in the War of Independence.* New York: Greenwood Press, October 1988.

Hyma, Albert. *Sir Henry Clinton and the American Revolution.* Ann Arbor, Michigan: Hyma, 1957.

Newcomb, Benjamin H. "Clinton, Sir Henry (1730–1795)." *Oxford Dictionary of National Biography.* Oxford: Oxford University Press, September 2004.

Willcox, William B. *Portrait of a General: Sir Henry Clinton in the War of Independence.* New York: Alfred A Knopf, 1964.

SAMUEL GRAVES, ADMIRAL

Miller, Nathan. *Sea of Glory: The Continental Navy fights for Independence 1775–1783.* New York: David McKay, 1974.

WILLIAM HOWE, GENERAL

Alden, John R.. *The American Revolution: 1775–1783.* New York: Harper, 1954.

Alden, John R.. *A History of the American Revolution.* New York: Da Capo Press, 1989.

Anderson, Troyer S. *The Command of the Howe Brothers During the American Revolution.* New York and London: Oxford University Press, 1936.

Billias, George A. *George Washington's Generals.* New York: William Morrow, 1969.

Boatner, Mark M. *Encyclopedia of the American Revolution.* Mechanicsburg, Pennsylvania: Stackpole Books, 1994 [1966].

Brooks, Victor. *The Boston Campaign: April 1775–March 1776.* Conshohocken, Pennsylvania: Combined Publishing, 1999.

Broughton-Mainwaring, Rowland B. *Historical Record of the Royal Welch Fusiliers, Late the Twenty-Third Regiment, or, Royal Welsh Fusiliers (the Prince of Wales's Own Royal Regiment of Welsh Fusiliers) Containing an Account of the Formation of the Regiment in 1689, and of Its Subsequent Services* to 1889. London: Hatchards, 1889.

Chichester, Henry M. "Howe, William (1729–1814)." *Dictionary of National Biography*.Volume 28, London: Smith, Elder & Co., 1885–1900.

Cokayne, George E. *Complete Peerage of England, Scotland, Ireland, Great Britain and the United Kingdom, Extant, Extinct, or Dormant, Volume 4*. London: G. Bell and Sons, 1892.

Fleming, Thomas. *Washington's Secret War*. New York: HarperCollins, 2006.

Fredriksen, John C. *America's Military Adversaries: From Colonial Times to the Present*. Santa Barbara, California: ABC—CLIO, 2001.

Galloway, Joseph. "A reply to the observations of Lieut. Gen. Sir William Howe, on a pamphlet, entitled Letters to a nobleman: in which his misrepresentations are detected, and those letters are supported, by a variety of new matter and argument."London: G. Wilkie, 1780.

Griffith, Samuel B. *The War for American Independence: From 1760 to the Surrender at Yorktown in 1781*. Urbana, Illinois: University of Illinois Press, 2002.

Gruber, Ira. *The Howe Brothers and the American Revolution*. New York: Published for the Institute of Early American History and Culture at Williamsburg, Virginia by Atheneum Press, 1972.

Hadden, James M, Horatio Rogers, Guy C. Dorchester, John Burgoyne, and William Phillips. *Hadden's Journal and Orderly Books. A Journal Kept in Canada and upon Burgoyne's Campaign in 1776 and 1777.* Albany, New York: J. Musell's Sons, 1884.

Higginbotham, Don. *The War of American Independence: Military Attitudes, Policies, and Practice, 1763–1789.* New York: Macmillan, 1971.

Howe, W. H. "The narrative of Lieut. Gen. Sir Wm. Howe, in a committee of the House of commons, on the 29th of April, 1779, relative to his conduct, during the late command of the king's troops in North America: to which are added, some observations upon a pamphlet, entitled, Letters to a nobleman." London: H. Baldwin, 1780.

Ketchum, Richard M. *Saratoga: Turning Point of America's Revolutionary War.* New York: Henry Holt, 1997.

Martin, David G. *The Philadelphia Campaign: June 1777–July 1778.* Conshohocken, Pennsylvania: Combined Books, 1993.

McGuire, Thomas J. *The Philadelphia Campaign, Vol. I: Brandywine and the Fall of Philadelphia.* Mechanicsburg, Pennsylvania: Stackpole Books, 2006.

Moomaw, W. H. "The Denouement of General Howe's Campaign of 1777." *English Historical Review* 79, 312 (1964): 498–512.

Pocock, Tom. *Battle for Empire: The Very First World War, 1756–63.* London: Michael O'Mara Books, 1998.

Smith, David. *William Howe and the American War of Independence.* London: Bloomsbury Academic, 2015.

Trevelyan, George O. *The American Revolution, Part 1.* New York: Longmans, Green, and Co, 1898.

BRITISH MONARCH

GEORGE III, KING OF ENGLAND
Ayling, Stanley E. *George the Third.* London: Collins, 1972.

Benjamin, Lewis S. *Farmer George.* Holborn, London: Pitman and Sons, 1907.

Black, Jeremy. *George III: America's Last King.* New Haven, Connecticut, and London: Yale University Press, 2006.

Brooke, John. *King George III.* London: Constable, 1972.

Butterfield, Herbert. *George III and the Historians.* London: Collins, 1957.

Cannon, John. "George III (1738–1820)." *Oxford Dictionary of National Biography.* Volume 21. Oxford: Oxford University Press, 2004.

Cannon, John, and Ralph A. Griffiths. *The Oxford Illustrated History of the British Monarchy.* Oxford and New York: Oxford University Press, 1988.

Carretta, Vincent. *George III and the Satirists from Hogarth to Byron*. Athens, Georgia: University of Georgia Press, 1990.

Colley, Linda. *Britons: Forging the Nation 1707–1837*. New Haven, Connecticut: Yale University Press, 1992.

Ditchfield, G. M. *George III: An Essay in Monarchy*. Houndmills, Basingstoke, Hampshire, England; New York: Palgrave Macmillan, 2002.

Fraser, Antonia. *The Lives of the Kings and Queens of England*. London: Weidenfeld and Nicolson, 1975.

Hecht, J. Jean. "The Reign of George III in Recent Historiography." In Elizabeth C. Furber, ed. *Changing Views on British History: Essays on Historical Writing since 1939*, 206–234. Cambridge, Massachusetts: Harvard University Press, 1966.

Hibbert, Christopher. *George III: A Personal History*. New York: Basic Books, 1999.

King George III, Lord John S. Bute, and Sedgwick Romney (ed.). *Letters from George III to Lord Bute, 1756–1766*. London: Macmillan and Co., Ltd., 1939

May, Thomas E. *The Constitutional History of England Since the Accession of George the Third, 1760–1860*. 11th edition. London and New York: Longmans, Green and Co., 1896.

Medley, Dudley J. *A Student's Manual of English Constitutional History*. Oxford: B. H. Blackwell, 1898.

Namier, Lewis B. "King George III: A Study in Personality." In *Personalities and Power*. London: Hamish Hamilton, 1955.

O'Shaughnessy, Andrew J. "'If Others Will Not Be Active, I Must Drive': George III and the American Revolution." *Early American Studies*. 2, 1 (Spring 2004): iii, 1–46.

Pares, Richard. *King George III and the Politicians*. Oxford: Clarendon Press, 1953.

Reitan, E. A., ed. *George III, Tyrant or Constitutional Monarch?* Boston: D. C. Heath and Company, 1964.

Simms, Brendan, and Torsten Riotte. *The Hanoverian dimension in British History, 1714–1837*. Cambridge: Cambridge University Press, 2007.

Smith, Robert A. "Reinterpreting the Reign of George III." In Richard Schlatter, ed., *Recent Views on British History: Essays on Historical Writing since 1966*, 197–254. New Brunswick, New Jersey: Rutgers University Press, 1984.

Thomas, Peter D. G. "George III and the American Revolution." *History* 70, 228 (1985): 16–31.

Trevelyan, George. *George the Third and Charles Fox: The Concluding Part of the American Revolution*. New York: Longmans, Green, 1912.

Watson, J. Steven. *The Reign of George III, 1760–1815*. Oxford: Clarendon Press, 1960.

Weir, Alison. *Britain's Royal Families: The Complete Genealogy, Revised Edition*. London: Bodley Head, 1989.

CONFLICTS IN MASSACHUSETTS BAY COLONY BEFORE THE REVOLUTION

BOSTON MASSACRE

A Fair Account of the Late Unhappy Disturbance at Boston. London: B. White, 1770.

A Short Narrative of the Horrid Massacre. London: W. Bingley, 1770.

Adams, John, and L. H. Butterfield, ed. *Diary and Autobiography of John Adams*. Volume 2. Cambridge, Massachusetts: The Belknap Press of Harvard University Press, 1962.

Allison, Robert J. *The Boston Massacre*. Beverly, Massachusetts: Commonwealth Editions, 2006.

Archer, Richard. As If an Enemy's Country: The British Occupation of Boston and the Origins of Revolution. Oxford and New York: Oxford University Press, 2010.

Bailyn, Bernard. *The Ordeal of Thomas Hutchinson*. Cambridge, Massachusetts: Belknap Press of Harvard University Press, 1974.

Beier, Anne. *Crispus Attucks: Hero of the Boston Massacre*. 1st edition. New York: Rosen Publishing Group, 2004.

Cumming, William P., and Hugh F. Rankin. *The Fate of a Nation: The American Revolution through Contemporary Eyes*. London and New York: Phaidon Press, 1975.

Knollenberg, Bernhard. *Growth of the American Revolution, 1766–1775*. New York: Free Press, 1975.

Lansford, Tom, and Thomas E. Woods. *Exploring American History: From Colonial Times to 1877*. New York: Marshall Cavendish Reference, 2008.

Middlekauff, Robert. *The Glorious Cause: The American Revolution, 1763–1789*. New York: Oxford University Press, 2005.

Miller, John. *Origins of the American Revolution*. Palo Alto, California: Stanford University Press, 1957.

O'Connor, Thomas H. *The Hub: Boston Past and Present*. Boston: Northeastern University Press, 2001.

Reid, John P. "A Lawyer Acquitted: John Adams and the Boston Massacre." *American Journal of Legal History* 18, 3 (1974).

Ritter, Kurt W. "Confrontation as Moral Drama: The Boston Massacre in Rhetorical Perspective." *Southern Speech Communication Journal* 42, 1 (1977): 114–36.

Ross, Betsy M. "From Loyalist to Founding Father: The Political Odyssey of William Samuel Johnson." New York: Columbia University Press, 1980.

Wheeler, William B., Susan Becker, and Lorri Glover. *Discovering the American Past: A Look at the Evidence: to 1877.* Belmont, California: Cengage Learning, 2011.

York, Neil L. "Rival Truths, Political Accommodation, and the Boston 'Massacre.'" *Massachusetts Historical Review* 11 (2009): 57–95.

York, Neil L.. *The Boston Massacre: A History with Documents.* New York: Routledge, 2010.

Young, Alfred. "Revolution in Boston? Eight Propositions for Public History on the Freedom Trail." *The Public Historian* 25, 2 (Spring 2003): 17–41.

Zinn, Howard. *A People's History of the United States.* New York: HarperCollins, 1999.

Zobel, Hiller B. *The Boston Massacre.* New York: W.W. Norton & Company, 1970.

BOSTON TEA PARTY

Ammerman, David. *In the Common Cause: American Response to the Coercive Acts of 1774.* Charlottsville, Virginia: University Press of Virginia, 1974.

Burgan, Michael. *The Boston Tea Party.* Minneapolis, Minnesota: Compass Point Books, 2000.

Carp, Benjamin L. *Defiance of the Patriots: The Boston Tea Party and the Making of America.* New Haven, Connecticut: Yale University Press, 2010.

Currier, Nathaniel. *The Destruction of Tea at Boston Harbor*. Graphic. Roxbury, Massachusetts, Nathaniel Currier, 1846.

Forman, Samuel A. *Dr. Joseph Warren: The Boston Tea Party, Bunker Hill, and the Birth of American Liberty*. Gretna, Louisiana: Pelican Publishing Co., Inc., 2012.

Hull, Mary. *The Boston Tea Party in American History*. Springfield, New Jersey: Enslow Publishers, 1999.

Ketchum, Richard. *Divided Loyalties: How the American Revolution Came to New York*. New York: Henry Holt, 2002.

Labaree, Benjamin W. *The Boston Tea Party*. Boston: Northeastern University Press, 1979.

Maier, Pauline. *The Old Revolutionaries: Political Lives in the Age of Samuel Adams*. New York: Knopf, 1980.

Mortensen, Lori, and Gershom Griffith. *The Boston Tea Party*. Minneapolis, Minnesota: Picture Window Books, 2010.

Raphael, Ray. *Founding Myths: Stories That Hide Our Patriotic Past*. New York: The New Press, 2004.

Thomas, Peter D. G. *Tea Party to Independence: The Third Phase of the American Revolution, 1773–1776*. Oxford and New York: Clarendon Press; Oxford University Press, 1991.

Thomas, Peter D. G. *The Townshend Duties Crisis: The Second Phase of the American Revolution, 1767–1773*. Oxford and New York: Clarendon Press; Oxford University Press, 1987.

Unger, Harlow G. *American Tempest: How the Boston Tea Party Sparked a Revolution*. Cambridge, Massachusetts: Da Capo Press, 2011.

Young, Alfred F. *The Shoemaker and the Tea Party: Memory and the American Revolution*. Boston: Beacon Press, 1999.

BATTLES OF LEXINGTON AND CONCORD
Alden, John R. "Why the March to Concord?" *The American Historical Review* 49 (1944): 446–54.

Anderson, Fred, and Institute of Early American History and Culture (Williamsburg, Virginia). *A People's Army: Massachusetts Soldiers and Society in the Seven Years War*. Chapel Hill, North Carolina: University of North Carolina Press, 1984.

Barker, John, and Elizabeth E. Dana. *The British in Boston: Being the Diary of Lieutenant John Barker of the King's Own Regiment from November 15, 1774 to May 31, 1776*. Cambridge, Massachusetts: Harvard University Press, 1924.

Borneman, Walter R. *American Spring: Lexington, Concord, and the Road to Revolution*. New York: Little, Brown and Company, 2014.

Bradford, Charles H. *The Battle Road: Expedition to Lexington and Concord*. Fort Washington, Pennsylvania: Eastern National, 1996.

Burke, Edmund. (1775). "Speech on Conciliation with the Colonies, March 22, 1775." The Works of the Right Honourable Edmund Burke. 6 Volumes, London: Henry G. Bohn, 1854-1856.

Chidsey, Donald B. *The Siege of Boston: An On-the-Scene Account of the Beginning of the American Revolution*. New York: Crown, 1966.

Coburn, Frank W. *The Battle of April 19, 1775*. Lexington, Massachusetts: The Lexington Historical Society, 1922.

Davis, K. C. *America's Hidden History: Untold Tales of the First Pilgrims, Fighting Women, and Forgotten Founders Who Shaped a Nation*. New York: Smithsonian Books, 2008.

Emerson, Ralph W. "Emerson's Concord Hymn." National Park Service, 1837.

Emerson, Ralph W., and George W. Curtis. "Proceedings at the Centennial Celebration of Concord Fight, April 19, 1875." Town of Concord, Massachusetts, 1875.

Evelyn, W. Glanville, and Gideon D. Scull. *Memoir and Letters of Captain W. Glanville Evelyn, of the 4th regiment ("King's Own,") from North America, 1774–1776*. Oxford: Printed for Private Circulation by J. Parker and Co., 1879.

French, Allen. *The Day of Concord and Lexington, the Nineteenth of April, 1775*. Boston: Little, Brown, and Company, 1925.

Frothingham, R. *History of the Siege of Boston, and of the Battles of Lexington, Concord, and Bunker Hill. Also an Account of the Bunker Hill Monument. With Illustrative Documents*. Boston: Little, Brown, & Co., 1873.

Galvin, John R. *The Minute Men: The First Fight: Myths and Realities of the American Revolution*, Washington, DC: Pergamon-Brassey's International Defense Publisher, 1989.

Hurd, D. Hamilton. *History of Middlesex County, Massachusetts, Volume 1: With Biographical Sketches of Many of Its Pioneers and Prominent men. Middlesex CO. (Mass.)* J. W. Lewis and Co., 1890.

Journals of the Continental Congress, Vol. II, May 10–September 20, 1775. Washington, DC: Government Printing Office, 1905.

Journals of the House of Commons, Volume 35. London: John Dixcey Cornish 1775.

Lister, Jeremy. *Concord Fight, Being So Much of the Narrative of Ensign Jeremy Lister of the 10th Regiment of Foot as Pertains to His Services on the 19th of April, 1775, and to His Experiences in Boston during the Early Months of the Siege.* Cambridge, Massachusetts: Harvard University Press, 1931.

Massachusetts Provincial Congress. *A Narrative of the Excursion and Ravages of the King's Troops.* Worcester: Isaiah Thomas, 1775.

Moore, Frank. *The Diary of the Revolution: A Centennial Volume.* Hartford, Connecticut: J. B. Burr Publishing, 1876.

Morrissey, Brendan. *Boston 1775: The Shot Heard around the World.* Westport, Connecticut: Praeger, 1995.

Raphael, Ray, and Marie Raphael. *The Spirit of '74: How the American Revolution Began.* New York: New Press, 2015.

Revere, Paul. *Deposition of April 1775.* Boston: Massachusetts Historical Society, 1775.

Revere, Paul *Letter to Jeremy Belknap of January, 1798.* Boston: Massachusetts Historical Society, 1798.

Sawicki, James A. *Infantry Regiments of the US Army*. Dumfries, Virginia: Wyvern Publications, 1981.

Shy, John. *A People Numerous & Armed*. Ann Arbor, Michigan: University of Michigan Press, 1990.

Smith, Samuel A. *West Cambridge 1775*. Arlington, Massachusetts: Arlington Historical Society, 1874.

Stark, James H. *The Loyalists of Massachusetts and the Other Side of the American Revolution*. Boston: J. H. Stark, 1907.

Tourtellot, Arthur B. *Lexington and Concord: The Beginning of the War of the American Revolution*. New York: W. W. Norton, 1959.

Urban, Mark. *Fusiliers: Eight Years with the Red Coats in America*. London: Faber and Faber, 2007.

BATTLE OF BUNKER HILL

Brooks, Victor. *The Boston Campaign*. Conshohocken, Pennsylvania: Combined Publishing, 1999.

Chidsey, Donald B. *The Siege of Boston*. Boston: Crown, 1966.

French, Allen. *The Siege of Boston*. New York: McMillan, 1911.

Frothingham, Richard, Jr. *History of the Siege of Boston and of the Battles of Lexington, Concord, and Bunker Hill, Second Edition*. Boston: Charles C. Little and James Brown, 1851.

Ketchum, Robert. *Decisive Day: The Battle For Bunker Hill*. New York: Henry Holt and Co., 1999 [1974].

Philbrick, Nathaniel. *Bunker Hill: A City, a Siege, a Revolution*. New York: Viking, 2013.

AMERICAN REVOLUTION

Bailyn, Bernard. *The Ideological Origins of the American Revolution*. Cambridge, Massachusetts: Belknap Press of Harvard University Press, 1992.

Boatner, Mark M., III. *Encyclopedia of the American Revolution. Library of Military History*. New York: David McKay, 1975 [1964].

Boston 200 Corporation and Boston's Fourth of July Inc. *Boston Celebrates July '76*. Danbury, New Hampshire: Addison House, 1976.

Commager, Henry S. *Documents of American History*. 9th edition. Englewood Cliffs, New Jersey: Prentice-Hall, 1973.

Commager, Henry S., and Richard B. Morris. *The Spirit of Seventy-six: The Story of the American Revolution as Told by Participants*. 1st Da Capo Press edition. New York: Da Capo Press, 1995.

Cook, Jane H. *Stories of Faith and Courage from the Revolutionary War*. Chattanooga, Tennessee: God and Country Press, 2007.

Hogeland, William. *Declaration: The Nine Tumultuous Weeks when America Became Independent, May 1–July 4, 1776*. New York: Simon & Schuster, 2010.

Kennedy, Frances H., and Conservation Fund (Arlington, Virginia). *The American Revolution: A Historical Guidebook*. New York: Oxford University Press, 2014.

Nevins, Allan, and Henry S. Commager. *America: The Story of a Free People*. 4th edition. London: Oxford University Press, 1976.

Sparer, Phineas J., Henry S. Commager, Eric F. Goldman, and Ashley Montagu. *America: Heritage and Horizons*. Memphis, Tennessee: Memphis State University Press, 1976.

Wallenfeldt, Jeffrey H. *The American Revolution and the Young Republic, 1763 to 1816*. 1st edition. New York: Britannica Educational Pub. in association with Rosen Educational Services, 2012.

Weber, Michael. *The American Revolution*. Austin, Texas: Raintree Steck-Vaughn, 2000.

HONORED GUESTS IN BOSTON—GEORGE WASHINGTON, BENJAMIN FRANKLIN, AND ALEXANDER HAMILTON: FOUNDING FATHERS FROM VIRGINIA, PENNSYLVANIA, AND NEW YORK.

GEORGE WASHINGTON: COMMANDER-IN-CHIEF, CONTINENTAL ARMY, AND FIRST PRESIDENT OF THE UNITED STATES

Alden, John R. *George Washington, a Biography*. Norwalk, Connecticut: Easton Press, 1993.

Anderson, Fred. *Crucible of War: The Seven Years' War and the Fate of Empire in British North America, 1754–1766.* New York: Alfred A. Knopf, 2000.

Billias, George Athan. *George Washington's Opponents.* New York: William Morrow, 1969.

Brookhiser, Richard. *Founding Father: Rediscovering George Washington.* New York: Free Press, 1996.

Chernow, Ron. *Washington: A Life.* New York: Penguin Books, 2010.

Cunliffe, Marcus. *George Washington, Man and Monument.* Boston: Little, Brown, 1958.

Dalzell, Robert F., Jr., and Lee Baldwin Dalzell. *George Washington's Mount Vernon: At Home in Revolutionary America.* New York: Oxford University Press, 1998.

Elkins, Stanley M., and Eric McKitrick. *The Age of Federalism.* New York: Oxford University Press, 1995 [1993].

Ellis, Joseph J. *His Excellency: George Washington.* New York: Alfred A. Knopf, 2004.

Ferling, John E. *First of Men: A Life of George Washington.* New York: Oxford University Press, 2010.

Ferling, John E. *Setting the World Ablaze: Washington, Adams, Jefferson, and the American Revolution.* New York: Oxford University Press, 2000.

Fischer, David H. *Washington's Crossing*. New York: Oxford University Press, 2006.

Fishman, Ethan M., William D. Pederson, and Mark J. Rozell. *George Washington: Foundation of Presidential Leadership and Character*. Westport, Connecticut: Greenwood Publishing Group, 2001.

Flexner, James T. *George Washington: The Forge of Experience, 1732–1775*. Boston: Little, Brown, 1965.

Flexner, James T. *Washington: The Indispensable Man*. Boston: Little, Brown, 1974.

Ford, Worthington Chauncey, Gaillard Hunt, and John Clement Fitzpatrick. *Journals of the Continental Congress, 1774-1789: 1774*. Washington, D.C.: US Government Printing Office, 1904.

Freedman, Russell. *Washington at Valley Forge*. New York: Holiday House, 2008.

Freeman, Douglas S. *George Washington, a Biography*. Clifton, New Jersey: a.m. Kelley, 1975.

Gregg, Gary L., II, and Matthew Spalding, eds. *Patriot Sage: George Washington and the American Political Tradition*. Wilmington, Delaware: ISI Books, 1999.

Grizzard, Frank E., Jr. *George Washington: A Biographical Companion*. Santa Barbara, California: ABC-CLIO, 2002.

Higginbotham, Don. *George Washington: Uniting a Nation*. Lanham, Maryland: Rowman & Littlefield Publishers, 2002.

Higginbotham, Don. *The War of American Independence: Military Attitudes, Policies, and Practice, 1763–1789.* New York: Macmillan, 1971.

Hirschfeld, Fritz. *George Washington and Slavery: A Documentary Portrayal.* Columbia, Missouri: University of Missouri Press, 1997.

Jensen, Merrill. *The Articles of Confederation: An Interpretation of the Social-Constitutional History of the American Revolution, 1774–1781.* Madison, Wisconsin: University of Wisconsin Press, 1948.

Kazin, Michael, et al. *The Princeton Encyclopedia of American Political History.* 2 volumes. Princeton, New Jersey: Princeton University Press, 2009.

Kohn, Richard H. *Eagle and Sword: The Federalists and the Creation of the Military Establishment in America, 1783–1802.* New York: Free Press, 1975.

Lancaster, Bruce, and John H. Plumb. *The American Revolution.* New York: American Heritage Press, 1985.

Leckie, Robert. *George Washington's War: The Saga of the American Revolution.* New York: HarperCollins, 1993.

Lengel, Edward G. *General George Washington: A Military Life.* New York: Random House, 2005.

Lillback, Peter, and Jerry Newcombe. *George Washington's Sacred Fire.* Bryn Mawr, Pennsylvania: Providence Forum Press, 2006.

Middlekauff, Robert. *Washington's Revolution: The Making of America's First Leader.* New York: Alfred A. Knopf, 2015.

McCullough, David. *1776*. New York: Simon & Schuster, 2005.

O'Brien, Conor C. *First in Peace: How George Washington Set the Course for America*. Foreword by Christopher Hitchens. Cambridge, Massachusetts: Da Capo Press, 2009.

Parry, Jay A.; Andrew M. Sllison, W. Wkousen, and George Cleonashington. *The Real George Washington*. Washington, DC: National Center for Constitutional Studies, 1991.

Randall, Willard S. *George Washington: A Life*. New York: Henry Holt & Co., 1997.

Rasmussen, William M. S., and Robert S. Tilton. *George Washington: The Man behind the Myths*. Charlottesville, Virginia: University Press of Virginia, 1999.

Spalding, Matthew, and Patrick J. Garrity. *A Sacred Union of Citizens: George Washington's Farewell Address and the American Character*. Lanham, Maryland: Rowman and Littlefield, 2000.

Stewart, David O. *The Summer of 1787*. New York: Simon & Schuster, 2008.

Thompson, Mary. *"In the Hands of a Good Providence." Religion in the Life of George Washington*. Charlottesville, Virginia: University of Virginia Press, 2008.

Unger, Harlow G. *"Mr. President": George Washington and the Making of the Nation's Highest Office*. Boston: Da Capo Press, 2013.

Varg, Paul A. *Foreign Policies of the Founding Fathers*. East Lansing, Michigan: Michigan State University Press, 1963.

Washington, Austin. *The Education of George Washington: How a Forgotten Book Shaped the Character of a Hero*. Washington, DC: Regnery Publishing Inc., 2014.

Washington, George. *George Washington Papers, 1592–1943* (bulk 1748–1799) Manuscript Division, Library of Congress, Washington D.C..

Washington, George, and Hon. Robert Dinwiddie. *The Journal of Major George Washington*. New York: Reprinted for J. Sabin, 1865.

White, Leonard D. *The Federalists: A Study in Administrative History*. New York: Macmillan Co., 1948.

Wood, Gordon S. *The Radicalism of the American Revolution*. New York: Alfred A. Knopf, 1992.

Wright, Robert K., and Morris J. MacGregor. "The Peace Establishment (George Washington, Sentiments on a Peace Establishment, 2 May 1783)." In *Soldier-Statesmen of the Constitution*. Carlisle Barracks, Pennsylvania: US. Army Center of Military History (U.S. Government), 1987.

BENJAMIN FRANKLIN: PUBLISHER, SCIENTIST, AND DIPLOMAT

Anderson, Douglas. *The Radical Enlightenments of Benjamin Franklin*. Baltimore, Maryland: Johns Hopkins University Press, 1997.

Asimov, Isaac. *The Kite That Won the Revolution.* Boston: Houghton Mifflin, 1963.

Brands, H. W. *The First American: The Life and Times of Benjamin Franklin.* New York: Doubleday, 2000.

Buxbaum, Melvin H., ed. *Critical Essays on Benjamin Franklin.* Boston: G. K. Hall, 1987.

Chaplin, Joyce. *The First Scientific American: Benjamin Franklin and the Pursuit of Genius.* New York: Basic Books, 2007.

Cohen, I. Bernard. *Benjamin Franklin's Science.* Cambridge, Massachusetts: Harvard University Press, 1990.

Conner, Paul W. *Poor Richard's Politicks: Benjamin Franklin and His New American Order.* New York: Oxford University Press, 1965.

Dray, Philip. *Stealing God's Thunder: Benjamin Franklin's Lightning Rod and the Invention of America.* New York: Random House, 2005.

Dull, Jonathan. *Benjamin Franklin and the American Revolution.* Lincoln, Nebraska: University of Nebraska Press, 2010.

Dull, Jonathan. *Franklin the Diplomat: The French Mission.* Independence Square, Philadelphia: American Philosophical Society, 1982.

Fleming, Candace. *Ben Franklin's Almanac: Being a True Account of the Good Gentleman's Life.* New York: Atheneum Books for Young Readers, 2003.

Ford, Paul L. "Franklin as Politician and Diplomatist." *The Century* 57 (October 1899): 881–99.

Ford, Paul L. "Franklin as Scientist." *The Century* 57 (September 1899): 750–63.

Ford, Paul L., and Benjamin Franklin Collection (Library of Congress). *The Many-Sided Franklin*. New York: The Century Co., 1899.

Franklin, Benjamin, and Alan C. Houston. *Franklin: The Autobiography and Other Writings on Politics, Economics, and Virtue*. Cambridge and New York: Cambridge University Press, 2004.

Franklin, Benjamin, and Walter Isaacson. *A Benjamin Franklin Reader*. New York: Simon & Schuster, 2003.

Franklin, Benjamin, and Ralph Ketcham. *The Political Thought of Benjamin Franklin*. Indianapolis, Indiana: Bobbs-Merrill, 1965.

Franklin, Benjamin, and Leonard W. Labaree, William B. Willcox, and Barbara Oberg. *The Papers of Benjamin Franklin*. New Haven, Connecticut: Yale University Press, 1959.

Franklin, Benjamin, and J. A. Leo Lemay. *Autobiography, Poor Richard, and Later Writings: Letters from London, 1757–1775, Paris, 1776–1785, Philadelphia, 1785–1790, Poor Richard's Almanack, 1733–1758: The Autobiography*. New York: Library of America, 1997.

Franklin, Benjamin, and J. A. Leo Lemay. *Silence Dogood, the Busy-Body, and Early Writings: Boston and London, 1722–1726, Philadelphia, 1726–1757, London, 1757–1775*. New York: Library of America, Penguin Putnam, 2002.

Franklin, Benjamin, and J. A. Leo Lemay and Paul M. Zall. *Benjamin Franklin's Autobiography: An Authoritative Text, Backgrounds, Criticism.* New York: W. W. Norton, 1986.

"Franklin as Printer and Publisher." *The Century* 57 (April 1899): 803–18.

Gleason, Philip. "Trouble in the Colonial Melting Pot." *Journal of American Ethnic History* 20, 1 (2000): 3–17.

Houston, Alan C. *Benjamin Franklin and the Politics of Improvement.* New Haven, Connecticut: Yale University Press, 2008.

Houston, Alan C, ed. *Franklin: The Autobiography and Other Writings on Politics, Economics, and Virtue.* Cambridge: Cambridge University Press, 2004.

Isaacson, Walter *Benjamin Franklin: An American Life.* New York: Simon & Schuster, 2003.

Ketcham, Ralph, ed. *The Political Thought of Benjamin Franklin.* Indianapolis, Indiana: Bobbs-Merrill, 1965.

Lemay, J. A. L. *Reappraising Benjamin Franklin: A Bicentennial Perspective.* Newark, London; Cranbury, New Jersey: University of Delaware Press; Associated University Presses, 1993.

Mathews, L. K. "Benjamin Franklin's Plans for a Colonial Union, 1750–1775." *American Political Science Review* 8 (August 1914): 393–412.

McCoy, Drew R. "Benjamin Franklin's Vision of a Republican Political Economy for America." *William and Mary Quarterly* 35, 4 (1978): 607–628.

Newman, Simon P. "Benjamin Franklin and the Leather-Apron Men: The Politics of Class in Eighteenth-Century Philadelphia." *Journal of American Studies* 43, 2 (August 2009): 161–75.

Olson, Lester C. *Benjamin Franklin's Vision of American Community: A Study in Rhetorical Iconology.* Columbia, South Carolina: University of South Carolina Press, 2004.

Schiff, Stacy. *A Great Improvisation: Franklin, France, and the Birth of America.* New York: Henry Holt, 2005.

Schiffer, Michael B., Kacy L. Hollenback, and Carrie L. Bell. *Draw the Lightning Down: Benjamin Franklin and Electrical Technology in the Age of Enlightenment.* Berkeley, California: University of California Press, 2003.

Skemp, Sheila L. *Benjamin and William Franklin: Father and Son, Patriot and Loyalist.* Boston: Bedford Books of Saint Martin's Press, 1994.

Sletcher, Michael. "Domesticity: The Human Side of Benjamin Franklin." *Magazine of History* XX (2006): 45-59.

Srodes, James. *Franklin, the Essential Founding Father.* Washington, DC: Regnery Pub., 2002.

Van Doren, Carl. *Benjamin Franklin.* New York: The Viking Press, 1938.

Waldstreicher, David. *Runaway America: Benjamin Franklin, Slavery, and the American Revolution.* New York: Hill and Wang, 2004.

Wood, Gordon S. *The Americanization of Benjamin Franklin*. New York: Penguin Press, 2004.

Wright, Esmond. *Franklin of Philadelphia*. Cambridge, Massachusetts: Belknap Press of Harvard University Press, 1986.

York, Neil. "When Words Fail: William Pitt, Benjamin Franklin and the Imperial Crisis of 1766." *Parliamentary History* 28, 3 (October 2009): 341–74.

ALEXANDER HAMILTON, FATHER OF UNITED STATES FEDERALIST ECONOMIC SYSTEM

Ambrose, Douglas, and Robert W. Martin. *The Many Faces of Alexander Hamilton: The Life and Legacy of America's Most Elusive Founding Father*. New York: New York University Press, 2006.

Bailey, Ralph E. *An American Colossus: The Singular Career of Alexander Hamilton*. Boston: Lothrop, Lee & Shepard Co., 1933.

Brookhiser, Richard. *Alexander Hamilton, American*. New York: Free Press, 1999.

Chernow, Ron. *Alexander Hamilton*. New York: Penguin Press, 2004.

Cooke, Jacob E. *Alexander Hamilton*. New York: Charles Scribner's Sons, 1982

Cooke, Jacob E, ed. *Alexander Hamilton: A Profile*. New York: Hill and Wang, 1967.

Cunningham, Noble E. *Jefferson vs. Hamilton: Confrontations That Shaped a Nation.* Boston: Bedford/Saint Martin's, 2000.

Derthick, M. *Dilemmas of Scale in America's Federal Democracy.* Washington, DC.: Woodrow Wilson Center Press, 1999.

Elkins, Stanley, and Eric McKitrick. *The Age of Federalism.* New York: Oxford University Press, 1993.

Emery, Noemie. *Alexander Hamilton: An Intimate Portrait.* New York: Putnam, 1982.

Engerman, Stanley L., and Robert E. Gallman. *The Cambridge Economic History of the United States.* Cambridge and New York: Cambridge University Press, 2000.

Fatovic, Clement. "Constitutionalism and Presidential Prerogative: Jeffersonian and Hamiltonian Perspectives." *American Journal of Political Science* 48, 3 (2004): 429–44.

Federici, Michael P. *The Political Philosophy of Alexander Hamilton.* Baltimore, Maryland: Johns Hopkins University Press, 2012.

Flaumenhaft, Harvey. *The Effective Republic: Administration and Constitution in the Thought of Alexander Hamilton.* Durham, North Carolina: Duke University Press, 1992.

Flexner, James T. *The Young Hamilton: A Biography.* Boston: Little, Brown, 1978.

Freeman, Joanne B. *Affairs of Honor: National Politics in the New Republic*. New Haven, Connecticut: Yale University Press, 2001.

Hamilton, Alexander, and Joanne B. Freeman (ed.). *Alexander Hamilton: Writings*. New York: Library of America, 2001.

Hamilton, Alexander, and Morton J. Frisch (ed.). *Selected Writings and Speeches of Alexander Hamilton*. Cambridge, Massachusetts: AEI Press, 1985.

Hamilton, Alexander, and Julius Goebel and Joseph H. Smith. *The Law Practice of Alexander Hamilton: Documents and Commentary*. New York: William Nelson Cromwell Foundation, Columbia University Press, 1964.

Hamilton, Alexander, and John C. Hamilton. *The Works of Alexander Hamilton: Miscellanies, 1789–1795: France; Duties on Imports; National Bank; Manufactures; Revenue Circulars; Reports on Claims, etc.* New York: John F. Trow, Printer, 1850.

Hamilton, Alexander, and Henry C. Lodge (ed.). *The Works of Alexander Hamilton*. New York and London: G. P. Putnam's Sons, 1904.

Hamilton, Alexander, James Madison, and John Jay, and Roy P. Fairfield. *The Federalist Papers: A Collection of Essays Written in Support of the Constitution of the United States: From the Original Text of Alexander Hamilton, James Madison, John Jay*. Baltimore, Maryland: Johns Hopkins University Press, 1981.

Hamilton, Alexander, and Harold C. Syrett and Jacob E. Cooke. *The Papers of Alexander Hamilton*. New York: Columbia University Press, 1961.

Hamilton, John C. *The Life of Alexander Hamilton*. New York: Halsted & Voorhies, 1834.

Harper, John L. *American Machiavelli: Alexander Hamilton and the Origins of US Foreign Policy*. New York: Cambridge University Press, 2004.

Hendrickson, Robert. *Hamilton*. New York: Mason/Charterre, 1976.

Kennedy, Roger G. *Burr, Hamilton, and Jefferson: A Study in Character*. New York: Oxford University Press, 2000.

Lind, Michael. "Hamilton's Legacy." *The Wilson Quarterly* 18, 3 (1994): 40–52.

Martin, Robert W. T. "Reforming Republicanism: Alexander Hamilton's Theory of Republican Citizenship and Press Liberty." *Journal of the Early Republic* 25, 1 (2005): 21–46.

McCraw, Thomas K. *The Founders and Finance: How Hamilton, Gallatin, and Other Immigrants Forged a New Economy*. Cambridge, Massachusetts: Belknap Press, 2012.

McDonald, Forrest. *Alexander Hamilton: A Biography*. New York: W. W. Norton Company, 1982.

Miller, John C. *Alexander Hamilton: Portrait in Paradox*. New York: Harper & Row, 1959.

Mitchell, Broadus. *Alexander Hamilton*. New York: Macmillan, 1957.

Mitchell, Broadus. "The Man Who 'Discovered' Alexander Hamilton." *Proceedings of the New Jersey Historical Society* 69 (1951): 88–115.

Morton, Joseph C. *Shapers of the Great Debate at the Constitutional Convention of 1787: A Biographical Dictionary.* Westport, Connecticut: Greenwood Press, 2005.

Murray, Joseph A., and ebrary Inc. *Alexander Hamilton: America's Forgotten Founder.* New York: Algora Pub., 2007.

Nester, William R. *The Hamiltonian Vision, 1789–1800: The Art of American Power during the Early Republic.* Sterling, Virginia: Potomac Books, 2012.

Nettels, Curtis P. *The Emergence of a National Economy, 1775–1815.* New York: Holt, Rinehart and Winston, 1962.

Newton, Michael E. *Alexander Hamilton: The Formative Years.* Phoenix, Arizona: Eleftheria Publishing, 2015.

Northup, Cynthia C., and Elaine C. Prange Turney, ed. *Encyclopedia of Tariffs and Trade in US History.* Westport, Connecticut: Greenwood Press, 2003.

Rakove, Jack N. *The Beginnings of National Politics: An Interpretive History of the Continental Congress.* New York: Knopf, 1979.

Randall, Willard S. *Alexander Hamilton: A Life.* New York: Harper Perennial Modern Classics, 2003.

Rossiter, Clinton L. *Alexander Hamilton and the Constitution.* New York: Harcourt, Brace & World, 1964.

Schachner, Nathan. *Alexander Hamilton.* New York and London: D. Appleton- Century Company, 1946.

Sharp, James R. *American Politics in the Early Republic: The New Nation in Crisis*. New Haven, Connecticut: Yale University Press, 1993.

Sheehan, Colleen. "Madison v. Hamilton: The Battle over Republicanism and the Role of Public Opinion." *American Political Science Review* 98, 3 (2004): 405–24.

Smith, Robert W. *Keeping the Republic: Ideology and Early American Diplomacy*. DeKalb, Illinois: Northern Illinois University Press, 2004.

Staloff, Darren. *Hamilton, Adams, Jefferson: The Politics of Enlightenment and the American Founding*. New York: Hill and Wang, 2005.

Stourzh, Gerald. *Alexander Hamilton and the Idea of Republican Government*. Palo Alto, California: Stanford University Press, 1970.

Studenski, Paul, and Herman E. Krooss. *Financial History of the United States*. 5th edition. Frederick, Maryland: Beard Books, 2003.

Sylla, Richard, Robert E. Wright, and David J. Cowen. "Alexander Hamilton, Central Banker: Crisis Management during the United States Financial Panic of 1792." *Business History Review* 83, 1 (2009): 61–86.

Taylor, George R., ed. *Hamilton and the National Debt*. Boston: Heath, 1950.

Thomas, Charles M. *American Neutrality in 1793: A Study in Cabinet Government*. New York: Columbia University Press, 1931.

Trees, Andrew S. *The Founding Fathers and the Politics of Character.* Princeton, New Jersey: Princeton University Press, 2004.

Tucker, Spencer C., ed. *The Encyclopedia of the Wars of the Early American Republic, 1783–1812.* 3 volumes. Santa Barbara, California: ABC-CLIO, 2014.

White, Leonard D. *The Federalists: A Study in Administrative History.* New York: Macmillan, 1948.

White, Richard D. "Exploring the Origins of the American Administrative State: Recent Writings on the Ambiguous Legacy of Alexander Hamilton." *Public Administration Review* 60, 2 (2000): 186–90.

Wood, Gordon S. *Empire of Liberty: A History of the Early Republic, 1789–1815.* New York: Oxford University Press, 2009.

Wright, Robert E., and ebrary Inc. *Hamilton Unbound: Finance and the Creation of the American Republic.* Westport, Connecticut: Greenwood Press, 2002.

DOWNTOWN BOSTON AND THE HARBOR

SCHOOL STREET
Andros, Howard S. *Buildings and Landmarks of Old Boston: A Guide to the Colonial, Provincial, Federal, and Greek Revival Periods, 1630–1850.* Lebanon, New Hampshire: University Press of New England, 2001.

The Boston Almanac. Boston: J. P. Jewett, 1862.

Carver, R., and Lilly, Wait, Colman & Holden. *History of Boston.* Boston: Lilly, Wait, Colman, and Holden, 1834.

Jenks, Henry F. "Old School Street." *New England Magazine* 13 (1895).

Kyle, George A. *The Eighteen Fifties: Being a Brief Account of School Street, the Province House and the Boston Five Cents Savings Bank.* Boston: Boston Five Cents Savings Bank, 1926.

School Street. *A Record of the Streets, Alleys, Places, etc. in the City of Boston.* City of Boston, 1910.

Ticknor, Caroline. *Hawthorne and His Publisher.* Boston: Houghton Mifflin, 1913.

DOWNTOWN CROSSING

Allison, Robert J. *A Short History of Boston.* Beverly, Massachusetts: Commonwealth Editions, 2004.

Boston Almanac and Business Directory. 1887, 1894.

Boston Directory. 1854.

Cassidy, Tina. "Area Codes: The Ladder District Has as Many Definitions of Proper Dress as It Does Hot New Nightspots." *Boston Globe* (November 17, 2001): F.1.

Cassidy, Tina "The Ladder District Is Looking Up." *Boston Globe* (June 11, 2006): H.1.

Elson, Louis. C., and Arthur Elson. *The History of American Music*. New York: B. Franklin, 1971.

Elson, Louis C.; Elson, Arthur *The History of American Music: With Twelve Full Page Photogravures and One Hundred and Two Illustrations in the Text*. New York: Macmillan Co., 1971.

Elson, Louis. C. *Elson's Music Dictionary*. Boston and New York: O. Ditson Company; C.H. Ditson and Co, 1905.

Elson, Arthur. *Woman's Work in Music*. Boston: L.C. Page & Company, 1904.

Goodison, Donna. "N.Y. Firm to Nab 17 Filene's Basement Stores for $22M." *Boston Herald* (May 5, 2009).

King, Moses. *King's Hand-book of Boston*. Cambridge, Massachusetts: M. King, 1885.

King's Hand-book of Boston. Cambridge, Massachusetts: M. King, 1889.

Mattero, Sarah. "Restored Modern Theater Finally Opens Its Doors." *The Suffolk Voice* (November 5, 2010).

New Music Hall. *Gleason's Pictorial*. Boston: 1852.

Orpheum Theatre, Hamilton Place. *Boston Register and Business Directory*. 1918.

Palmer, Thomas C., Jr. "Filene's Project to Feature a High-Rise; Condos, Offices, Hotel, Stores Part of Plan in Downtown Crossing." *Boston Globe*. (September 29, 2006): E.1.

Sammarco, Anthony M. *Images of America: Boston's Back Bay*. Mount Pleasant, South Carolina: Arcadia Publishing, 2012.

Shand-Tucci, Douglass. *Built in Boston: City and Suburb 1800–1950*. Amherst, Massachusetts, University of Massachusetts Press, 1988.

Tatham, David. "A Drawing by Winslow Homer: Corner of Winter, Washington and Summer Streets." *American Art Journal* 18, 3 (Summer 1986): 40–50.

""The Rebuilding of Boston. One Year after the Great Fire." November 10, 1872 *Boston Morning Journal* XL, 13 (November 10, 1873): 509.

ALEXANDER GRAHAM BELL

Bell, Alexander G. "On the Production and Reproduction of Sound by Light." *American Journal of Science* 20, 118 (October 1880): 305–324.

Bell, Alexander G. "Selenium and the Photophone." *Nature* 22 (September 23, 1880): 500–503.

Bell, Alexander G. The Question of Sign-Language and the Utility of Signs in the Instruction of the Deaf. "Washington, DC: Sanders Printing Office, 1898.

Bell, Mabel. "Dr. Bell's Appreciation of the Telephone Service." *Bell Telephone Quarterly* 1, 3 (October 1922): 65.

Bruce, Robert V. *Bell: Alexander Bell and the Conquest of Solitude.* Ithaca, New York: Cornell University Press, 1990.

Carson, Mary K. *Alexander Graham Bell: Giving Voice to the World.* Sterling Biographies. New York: Sterling Publishing, 2007.

Gray, Charlotte. *Reluctant Genius: The Passionate Life and Inventive Mind of Alexander Graham Bell.* New York: Arcade, 2006.

Grosvenor, Edwin S., and Morgan Wesson. *Alexander Graham Bell: The Life and Times of the Man Who Invented the Telephone.* New York: Harry N. Abrams, 1997.

Mackay, James. *Sounds out of Silence: A Life of Alexander Graham Bell.* Edinburgh, United Kingdom: Mainstream Publishing, 1997.

MacKenzie, Catherine D. *Alexander Graham Bell.* Boston: Grosset and Dunlap, 1928.

Mackenzie, Catherine D. *Alexander Graham Bell, the Man Who Contracted Space.* Boston and New York: Houghton Mifflin Company, 1928.

Matthews, Tom L. *Always Inventing: A Photobiography of Alexander Graham Bell.* Washington, DC: National Geographic Society, 1999.

Mims III, Forest M. "The First Century of Lightwave Communications". *Fiber Optics Weekly Update. Information Gatekeepers* 11 (February 10–26, 1982): 6–23.

Osborne, Harold S. "Biographical Memoir of Alexander Graham Bell 1847–1922." *Biographical Memoirs. Vol. XXIII,* 18. Whitefish, Montana: National Academy of Sciences, 1943.

Petrie, A. Roy. *Alexander Graham Bell.* Don Mills, Ontario: Fitzhenry & Whiteside, 1975.

Ross, Stewart. *Alexander Graham Bell (Scientists Who Made History).* New York: Raintree Steck-Vaughn, 2001.

Shulman, Seth. *The Telephone Gambit: Chasing Alexander Bell's Secret.* New York: W. W. Norton & Co., 2008.

Webb, Michael, ed. *Alexander Graham Bell: Inventor of the Telephone.* Mississauga, Ontario: Copp Clark Pitman, 1991.

Wing, Chris. *Alexander Graham Bell at Baddeck.* Baddeck, Nova Scotia: Christopher King, 1980.

THE FINANCIAL DISTRICT

Gras, Norman S. B. *The Massachusetts First National Bank of Boston, 1784–1934.* Cambridge, Massachusetts: Harvard University Press, 1937.

Menzies, Ian. "New Federal Reserve Building Gives Dull Area Sparkling Face." *Boston Globe* (June 1, 1977): 19.

"One Beacon Street Story." *Boston Globe* (March 21, 1971): A. 11.

Sege, Irene. "Bank of Boston Announces Its Gift of $1.5 M to Endow Hub's Schools." *Boston Globe* (February 8, 1984): 1.

Spencer, C. E. *The First Bank of Boston, 1784–1949*. New York: Newcomen Society in North America, 1949.

Williams, Ben A. *Bank of Boston 200: A History of New England's Leading Bank, 1784–1984*. Boston: Houghton Mifflin, 1984.

Yudis, Anthony. "Bank Skyscraper to Rise Downtown." *Boston Globe* (June 25, 1966): 23.

Yudis, Anthony "First National Bank Plans 37-Story Building-with-a-Bulge." *Boston Globe* (July 30, 1967): 26.

POST OFFICE SQUARE, ART DECO DESIGN AND ARCHITECTURE

Arwas, Victor, and Frank D. Russell. *Art Deco*. New York: Harry N. Abrams Inc., 1980.

Bayer, Patricia. *Art Deco Architecture: Design, Decoration and Detail from the Twenties and Thirties*. New York: Thames & Hudson, 1999.

Benton, Charlotte, Tim Benton, Ghislaine Wood, and Oriana Baddeley. *Art Deco: 1910–1939*. Boston: Bulfinch Press, 2003.

Breeze, Carla. *American Art Deco: Architecture and Regionalism*. New York: W. W. Norton, 2003.

Charles, Victoria; Carl, Klaus H.; ebrary Inc. *Art Déco*. New York: Parkstone Press International, 2013.

Duncan, Alastair. *Art Déco*. Holborn, London: Thames & Hudson, 1988.

Duncan, Alastair *Art Deco Complete: The Definitive Guide to the Decorative Arts of the 1920s and 1930s*. New York: Harry N. Abrams, Inc., 2009.

"Federal Reserve Bank Buys Site for New Banking House. *Boston Daily Globe* (August 30, 1919): 3.

Gallagher, Fiona. *Christie's Art Deco*. New York: Watson-Guptill Publications, 2000.

Hillier, Bevis. *Art Deco of the 20s and 30s*. London: Studio Vista, 1968.

Long, Christopher. *Paul T. Frankl and Modern American Design*. New Haven, Connecticut: Yale University Press, 2007.

Lucie-Smith, Edward. *Art Deco Painting*. New York: Phaidon Press, 1996.

Morel, Guillaume. *Art Déco (in French)*. Paris: Éditions Place des Victoires, 2012.

Okroyan, Mkrtich. *Art Deco Sculpture: From Root to Flourishing*. 2 volumes. Moscow: Russian Art Institute, 2011.

Plum, Giles. *Paris architectures de la Belle Epoque* (in French). Paris: Parigramme, 2014.

Poisson, Michel. *1000 Immeubles et monuments de Paris: dictionnaire visuel des architectes de la capitale* (in French). Paris: Parigramme, 2009.

Ray, Gordon N. and G. Thomas Tansell (ed.). *The Art Deco Book in France*. Charlottesville, Virginia: Bibliographical Society of the University of Virginia, 2005.

Texier, Simon. *Paris, panorama de l'architecture de l'antiquité à nos jours*. Paris: Parigramme, 2012.

Unes, Wolney. *Identidade art déco de Goiânia*. São Paulo, Goiânia: Ateliê Editorial; Universidade Federal de Goiás, 2001.

Vincent, Gregory K. *A History of Du Cane Court: Land, Architecture, People and Politics*. New York: Woodbine Press, 2008.

Ward, Mary, and Neville Ward. *Home in the Twenties and Thirties*. London: Ian Allan, 1978.

BOSTON HARBOR

Harbor Islands Study Group., and Massachusetts Boston Harbor Islands Commission. *The Harbor Islands*. Commonwealth of Massachusetts, 1969.

Jones, Laura T. *Generations 1891–1940: Living on the Islands of Boston Harbor*. Bloomington, Indiana: AuthorHouse, 2011.

Kales, David. *Boston Harbor Islands: A History of Urban Wilderness*. Charleston, South Carolina: History Press, 2007.

Lamb, Thomas, and YA Pamphlet Collection (Library of Congress). *Plan and Suggestions for Improving Boston Harbor and, Incidentally, the Vicinity.* Boston: E. P. Dutton, 1867.

Levering, Dale, and Olga Pastuchiv. *An Illustrated Flora of the Boston Harbor Islands.* Boston: Northeastern University Press, 1978.

Lownes, Caleb. *A New Plan of Boston Harbour from an Actual Survey.* Philadelphia: 1775.

Perkins, William D. *Chestnuts, Galls, and Dandelion Wine: Useful Wild Plants of the Boston Harbor Islands.* Halifax, Massachusetts: Plant Press, 1982.

Snow, E. R. *The Islands of Boston harbor, 1630–1971.* New York: Dodd, 1971.

Tenney (W. M.) & Co. "Map of Boston harbor showing islands, shoals, channels, buoys, lighthouses, and ledges from Nahant to Minot's Light." Boston: 1885.

Wheeler, Thomas, James Grant, and Samuel Holland. "A plan of the bay and harbor of Boston, surveyed agreeably to the orders and instructions of the right honorable the lords commissioners for trade and plantations, to Samuel Holland, esqr., His Majesty's surveyor general of lands for the northern district of North America." 1775.

OLD CITY HALL AND NEW CITY HALL

Bartnick, Harry. "Could City Hall Be Literally Transparent?" *Boston Globe* (July 26, 2015): K.4.

Campbell, Robert. "Ugly Is in the Eye of the Beholder." *Boston Globe* (March 21, 2010): N. 7.

Casey, Ross. "A 10-Year Plan for City Hall Plaza: New Incremental Approach Starts with Remodeled T Station, Trees." *Boston Globe* (March 16, 2011): B.7.

"Panoramic view of Boston City Hall, School Street," (photographic print). Boston: E. Chickering & Co., 1903.

McMorrow, Paul. "Tear Down City Hall." *Boston Globe* (September 24, 2013): A.13.

Millard, Charles W. "The New Boston: City Hall." *The Hudson Review* 23, 1 (Spring 1970): 110–15.

Thomas, Jack. "'I Wanted Something That Would Last'; at 89, an Architect Stands by His Plan for City Hall after Four Decades of Both Condemnation and Praise." *Boston Globe* (October 13, 2004): E.1.

Shurtleff, Nathaniel B., Hammatt Billings, and Boston City Council, Benjamin Franklin Collection (Library of Congress). *Memorial of the Inauguration of the Statue of Franklin*. Boston: Prepared and Printed by Authority of the City Council, 1857.

OLD AND NEW MASSACHUSETTS STATE HOUSES

Bridgman, Arthur M. *A Souvenir of Massachusetts Legislators*. Stoughton, Massachusetts: A.M. Bridgman, 1908

Hitchings, Sinclair, Catherine H. Farlow, and John Hancock Mutual Life Insurance Company. *A New Guide to the Massachusetts State House.* Boston: John Hancock Mutual Life Insurance Company, 1964.

Hitchings, Sinclair, Catherine F. Hitchings, John DePol, and Boston Safe Deposit and Trust Company. *Theatre of Liberty: Boston's Old State House.* Boston: Boston Safe Deposit and Trust Co., 1975.

Kirker, Harold. *Architecture of Charles Bulfinch.* Cambridge, Massachusetts: Harvard University Press, 1969.

ABOUT THE AUTHOR

Physician and author Alan Balsam first became interested in writing about the history of Boston during and after the American bicentennial celebrations of 1976. At the time, he was working as a faculty member of Harvard Medical School and as a consultant with the Commonwealth of Massachusetts Disability Determination Services. In *A Boston Quartet*, Balsam combines his personal memory of the festivities with his thorough research into the history and environmental delights of the area.

Balsam has also published a number of noted medical articles as well as a full-length textbook, *Disability Handbook*.

INDEX

A

a beggar 78
A blind woman 76
Acer palmatum 124
Acer platanoides 124
Acer rubrum 124
Acer saccharinum 124
Acis 35
acorns 101,122
Acts of 1763 51
Administration of Justice Act 51
Aesculus hippocastanum 126
Alexander Graham Bell 77, 211,212,213
Alexander Hamilton 18,192,202, 203,204,205,206,207,208
Algonquian 24,25,26,161
American Colonies 63,81
American elm 125
American History 49,60,120, 146,164,165,170,178,184,186, 187,191
American Indian 24,94,161
American Revolution xv, xvi, xvii, 64,67,68,69,72,81,82,113, 143,167,168,169,170,174,175, 176,177,178,180,182,184,186, 187,188,189,190,191,192,193, 195,197,198,201
Ames Building 86
Amphitrite 35
Anne Hutchinson 81,163,164,166
Apollos Rivoire 59
Appalachian Mountains 52
Appeal to the Great Spirit 105

Arborway 2
architecture 7,11,13,44,45,84,87, 91,92,93,107,112,149,153,214, 215,216,219
Arlington Street 4,5, 16,17,19,22, 118,119,120,124,125
Arnold Arboretum 2,21
art deco 77,80,86,91,92,118,119, 214,215,216
Art Square 112
autumn 93,94,95,96,97,98,101,102, 105,116,121,122,123,126,127

B

Back Bay 1,2,4,5,6,7,8,9,10,11,12, 13,14,15,16,17,18,19,23,24,27, 30,31,54,78,94,97,98,99,100, 104,106,107,108,109,110,111, 113,114, 115,116,118,137,149, 150,152,153,211
Back Bay alley parking spaces 14
Bank of Boston 86,87,89,145,213,214
Bank of New England building 87
Battle of Bunker Hill 65,66,190
Battles of Lexington and Concord xvi,65,187,188,190
Beacon Hill 19,23,24,28,29,30,31, 32,34,35,37,39,40,44,57,80,132, 135,136,137,149,160,161,170

Beacon Street 5,6,19,23,28,29,30, 31,37,57,80, 98,124,125,136, 213,
Beaver 63
Beech 3,4,21,22,124,126
Beech Road 3,4
Belgian elm 125
Benjamin Franklin 80,81,90,192, 197,198,199,200,201,202,218
Berkeley Building 115
Berkeley Street 17,115,118,
Bibliotheque Nationale of Paris 111
Bicentennial xv,xvii, 29,37,42,56,75,86,87,89,91, 93,119,120,137,144,145,146, 200,221
Blizzard of 1978 138,139
Boreus 132
Boston xv,xvi, 1,5,6,7,8,9,12,16,18, 19,21,22,23,24,26,27,28,30, 32, 35,36,37,39,40,43,44,45, 46,47,48,49,53,54,55,57,58,59, 60,62,63,64,65,66,67,69,72,73, 75,76, 80,81,83,84,85,86,87, 88,89,90,91,92,93,94,95,97,98, 100, 105,106,107, 110,112,113, 114,115,116,118,119,120,121, 132,133, 140,141,142,144,145, 149,150,151,152,153,154,155, 156,157,158,159,160,161,162,

163,167,168,169,170,171,172,
173,174,177,182,183,184,185,
186,187,188,189,190,191,192,
193,194,196,198,199,201,202,
203,207,208,209,210,211,212,
213,214,215, 217,218,219,221
Boston Common 1,19,22,23,24,
26,27,28,30,31,32,34,35,
65,78,119,128,129,130,
133,134,136,142,146,157,
158,159
Boston Evening Clinic 9
Boston Massacre 53,62,
69,130,183,185
Boston Museum of Fine Arts 12,
104,105,107,112,113,114,150,
171
Boston Music Hall 77,78,106
Boston Pops 106
Boston post office 90
Boston Proper 7
Boston Public Garden 1,2,7,18,19,
20,21,22,23,31,39,40,94,97,98,
119,120,121,122,123,125,126,
134,137,155,156,158
Boston Public Library 109,110,
111,114
Boston Red Caps 73
Boston Red Stockings 73
Boston Symphony Orchestra
77,78,106

Boston Tea Party 60,63,64,185,
186,187
Boylston Street 5,6,16,19,20,23,
37,38,89,98,99,107,108,109,
111,117,118,119,120,123,125,152
Brahmins 7,58,85
Brewer Fountain 29,34,35,36,37
Brimmer and May School 99
British xv, xvi,7,19,27,50,53,54,
55,56,57,58,59,60,61,62,63,64,
65,66,67,68,69,70,71,72,143,
167,173,174,175,176,180,181,
182,183,187,193
Brookline 1,2,3,30,34,35,40,75,
98,100,101,107,150
Brookline Avenue 102
Brookline Village 3,102
Brooklyn Dodgers 73
brownstones 8,10,11,12,13,14,
16,118
brutalism 92
Building A 9
Bunker Hill xvi,65,66,186,188,
190,191
buntings 2
Burr oak 125

C

Calvinistic theology 47
Cambridge 6,7,26, 65,98,103,136,
149,153,155,156,157,159,161,

225

164,165,169,170,173,176,181,
182,183,187,189,190,191,196,
198,199,200,202,203,204,
205,210,213,219
Cambridge Agreement   55
Cambridge Street   29,30,44,136
Campanile   110
Camperdown elm   125
Canada geese   33,121
Cape Cod   26
Carl Erskine   73
carless in Back Bay   14,15
Castle William   62
Centennial Anniversary   xvi, 142,143,
centennial year   72,112,114
Central Burying Ground   28,38
Charles Bulfinch   28,30,219
Charles Follen McKim   111
Charles River   5,6,8,10,18,21, 24,137
Charles Street   19,22,23,28,29,118, 120,124,125,129,132
Charlesgate East   4,5,6
Charlestown   48,66
Charlestown Navy Yard   47
Charybdis   38,41
Chestnut Hill   1,2,3,98,101
Chestnut Hill Reservoir   3
Chestnut Hill School   99,101
Chestnut Hill T Station   97,100

Chestnut trees   99,126
Chestnuts   101,122,126,217
Chicago Cubs   73
Chicago White Stockings   73
Chinatown   37,41,42,44,77
Church of England   47
Clarendon Street   6,111,115
Claude Monet   105
Cocoanut Grove nightclub 119,120,159
Coercive and Intolerable Acts   51
Colonial Times   60,161,178,184
Commonwealth Avenue   1,2,4,5,6, 7,8,10,15,16,17,109,150
Commonwealth Mall   1,8,13, 15,18
Concord   xvi,64,65,70,97,187, 188,189,190
Congress Street   44,45,90
constructivism   91
Copley Place   108
Copley Square   100,104,105,106, 108,109,110,111,112,113,114, 116,153
cormorants   33
Corner Bookstore   81
Countway Medical Library   100, 102
Court Street   80,82
crows   33
cubism   91

Currency Act 51
Custom House Tower 86,92,115
Cyrus Dallin 105

D

Daffodils 1
Dartmouth 60,63
Dartmouth Street 16,17, 109,111,112,150
Deborah Hitchborn 59
deciduous 8,97,125,126
Declaration of Independence xv, xvi, 74,143
Disability Determination Services 77,221
dogwoods 1,8
Dorchester Heights 19,66,67
Downtown Boston 6,8,43,44,45, 46,47,75,83,84,88,90,100, 208,214
Downtown Crossing 44,46, 77,78,79,89,209,211
Downtown Skyscrapers 86
Dr. Murray Gavel 15
Dr. Watson 77
ducks 25,33,94,121

E

East India Company 63
eastern phoebes 32
Ebbets Field 73

Eleanor 63
Elizabeth Hooten 58
Elizabeth Stanton 74
elm 20,21,123,124,125,126,158
Emerald Necklace 1,2,40
Emerson xvi,81,188
England 48,49,55,56,61,63,67, 68,69,70,71
English elm 125
English heritage 48,69,72
English oak 125
equestrian statue of Washington 20
Esplanade 6
Essex Street 37
European beech 124
European starlings 33
Evacuation Day 66
Exeter Street 6,111

F

Fagus purpurea 124
Fagus sylvatica 124
Fagus sylvatica pendula 124
Fairmont Copley Plaza Hotel 114
Faneuil Hall 55
Father of American Liberty 56
Federal Reserve Bank Building 86,87,145,213
Fens 1,103

227

Fenway   3,103,104,105,114
Filene's department store   79, 210,211
Financial District   44,87,213
First Settlement in Massachusetts   47
Francis Bernard   173,174
Franklin Park   2
Franklin Roosevelt   90
Franklin Street   90,92
Freemasonry   57,59,173
French and Indian War   50, 53,59,166
French Second Empire style   16,80
Frog Pond   28,132
frontalism   12,92
functionalism   91
futurism   91

G

Galatea   35
Gardner Brewer   35
geese   33,94,121
General Joseph Hawley   74
George Berry Packer   103
George F. Meacham   19
George III   69,180,181,182
George Washington   18,19,66,175, 177,192,193,194,195,196,197
Georgian style   82,83

Gilbert Stuart   105
Giverny   105
Gorges expedition   26
Governor Hutchinson   63
grackles   33
Green Line   2,34,75,100,104
Griffin's Wharf   63

H

Halifax   19,50,54,217
Hamilton Place   77,106,210
Hammond Street   1,98,99
Hanover Street   58
Harbor   xvi, 21,26,27,28,33,44, 45,47,49,55,62,63,64,66,86,87, 145,186,208,216,217
Harvard College   49,55,57,58
Harvard Dental School   104
Harvard University   21,149,153, 161,165,169,170,173,181,183, 187,189,191,198,202,213,219
Hawthorne   81,209
Henry Clinton   65,176,177
Henry Cobb   115
Henry Hobson Richardson   112
Henry Statler   119
Hereford Street   8,9
High Street   44,81
Holland   47,48
Holmes   81
homeless population   37,42

horse chestnut tree   126
house sparrows   33
Huntington Avenue   100,102, 104,106,107,108,111,114
Huntington Avenue T   104

I
I. M. Pei & Associates   115
Independence   xv, xvi, xvii,8,24, 29,42,49,55,56,61,65,68,70,71, 72,73,74,81,112,142,143,167, 174,176,177,178,179,180,186, 195,198,
Indian summer   94
Indian winter   142
Interstate 93   45

J
Jamaica Plain   1,2,21,100
Jamaica Pond   1,2
Jamaicaway   2,107
Japanese larch tree   126
Japanese maple   124
Jean Liénard   35
Joe Borden   73
John Burgoyne   65,175,176,179
John Hancock   30,57,60,168, 169,170,219
John Hancock Tower   114,115, 117,153,154,155
John Singleton Copley   113,153

Jonathan Mayhew   51
Joseph Warren   58,59,66,81,171, 186
Joy Street   136,160

K
Kautantowwit   24
Kenmore Square   1,3,4,100
Kevin White   32
Kingfishers   32

L
Lagoon   20,121,123,125,155,156
Larix kaempferi   126
larks   32
Le Déjeuner sur l'Herbe   35
Leather District   37,41
Leiden   48
Lexington   xvi, 60,65,187, 188,190
Lexington Common   70
Liberty   57
lion and unicorn   93
little leaf lindens   21,99,118
London planes   109,118
Longfellow   81,82,172
Longfellow Bridge   29
Longwood Avenue   99,100, 102,104
Longwood T station   3,102
loons   33

Loyalists 7,54,61,65,190
Lydia Henchman Hancock 57

M

magnolias 1,8
maidenhair tree 22
Manet 35
Manhattan 43
mansion at the corner of Hereford Street 8,9
Marlborough Street 5,6,8,15
Martha Washington 105
martyrs 27,130
Mary Hawke Thaxter 57
Massachusett 98
Massachusetts Avenue 104
Massachusetts Bay Colony xv,xvi, 26,48,64,67,68,161,162,165, 166,173,175,183
Massachusetts Bay Transportation Authority 100
Massachusetts Government Act 51
Massachusetts Turnpike 5
Massasoit 26
MBTA 100
Men in Mohawk Indian dress 64
Mildam 5
Milk Street 46,81
modernism 91
Mohegan 26

molasses 50,52
Mount Pemberton 29
Mount Vernon 29,193
Mount Vernon Street 137,160

N

Nantucket 26
National League of Professional Baseball Clubs 73
National Woman Suffrage Association 74
natural habitat for birds 32
Nauset 26
Needham 5
Neptune 35
New City Hall 80,93,145,217
New England 19,25,32,48,94,95, 96,115,116,121,129,131,134,139, 141,156,158,160,162,163,165, 166,169,171,174,208,209,214
New England Life Insurance Building 118
New England Telephone Building 92
Newbury Street 4,5,11,16,108
Newe Towne 98
Newton 2,30,35,75,97,98,100, 101,107,114
Nipmuc 26
Nonantum 98
North End 26,28,44,45,59

northeastern gray squirrel   122
Norway maple   123,124
Nova Scotia   19,213

O

oak   21,25,99,102,125,126
Oak Hill   98
Old Burying Ground   80
Old City Hall   80,81,90,145,217
Old Ironsides   47
Old Post Office   90,91
Old South Church   109,110,153
Old South Meeting House   63,110
Old State House   28,30,82,83, 219
Old West Church   68
Olmstead Park   1
One Ashburton Place   137
One Beacon Place   47,213
One Exeter Place   109

P

pagoda tree   21,126
Park Square   18,117,118,119,120, 158,159
Park Square Station   118
Patrick Henry   53
Paul Revere   59,82,171,172,173
Pearl Street   90,92
Pennacook   26
People of the Sunrise (Wampanoag)   26
Pequot   26,150
peregrine falcon   34
Perkins School for the Blind   77
Peter Minuet   43
Philadelphia Athletics   73
pigeons   33
pileated woodpecker   2
Pilgrims   26,47,68,161,164,188
Pin oak   125
Plimoth Plantation   48
Plymouth   26,47,48,162
Pocasset   26
Pocumtuc   26
Pokanoket   26
Portland brownstone   12
Post Office Square   90,92,214
post-traumatic stress disorder   38
preservationism   13,14,15,84,85
Prudential Center   108
Prudential Tower   114
Puritans   26,27,28,35,47,48,49,55, 58,68,130,163,164,165

Q

Quakers   130
Quartering Act   54,56
quartering of British troops   53, 54
Quercus macrocarpa   125

Quercus palustris   125
Quercus robur   125

R

Rachel Walker   60
Radio City Music Hall   91
red maple   123,124
Renaissance style   106,111
Reverend John Hancock   57
Riverside branch   2,99
Riverway   1,2,3,102
Roaring Twenties   119
robins   33
Rolls-Royce   15
Romanesque Revival style   9
rose-breasted grosbeaks   32
Roxbury puddingstone   110
ruby-throated hummingbirds   33
rum   50,52,57

S

S. pendulina "elegantissima"   126
sachem   25,98
sagamores   25
Saint Anthony's Shrine   79
Saint James Street   107,111
Saint Louis Brown Stockings   73
Salix Babylonica   125
Salon des Refuses   35
Samuel Adams   55,58,60,167,168, 169,186

Samuel Graves   177
Samuel Gray   62
sandstone   12
Sara Andrews Spencer   74
Sarah Orne   59
School Street   30,37,80,81,82, 208,209,218
Scylla   38
seagulls   33
season of the trees   95
Second Continental Congress   xv, 66
Second Settlement in New England   48
shaman   25
Shawmut Peninsula   26,27,48,163
silver maple   123,124
snow   103,127,134,135,136,137, 138,139,141
Sons of Liberty   56,59,167,171
Sophora japonica   126
spring   1,2,4,8,22,32,41,95,96, 101,121,122,123,124,126,140, 141,142,146
squirrels   101,122,129
Stamp Act   51,53,69
standing army   53
State House   28,29,30,31,37,40, 57,82,83,137,218,219
State Street   28,82
State Street Bank building   86

Stephen L. Brown building   115
storms and stresses of winter   137
Storrow Drive   6
Sudbury Street   44
Suffragettes   74
Sugar Act   50,51
summer   4,22,23,24,32,33,36,43, 55,60,72,78,93,94,95,96,101, 112,119,121,122,123,124,128, 132,142,196
Susan B. Anthony   74
swallows   32
swan boats   21,155
Symphony Hall   78,106, 107

T

T stations   1,2,3,29,34,35,36,37, 75,76,89,97,99,100,102,153,218
tax levies   52
taxation without representation   63
tea acts   51
Theatre des Champs-Elysees   91
Thomas Alva Edison   111,117,151, 152,
Thomas Crease   81
Thomas Gage   64,65,175
Thomas Hancock   57
thrushes   32
Tilia cordata   99
Tories   7

Townshend Acts   54,62,63,169, 186
trade restrictions   xvi,52,57
Tremont Street   23,26,29,33,34, 37,45,76,80,118,119.129,132
Trinity Church   111,112

U

Ulmus Americana   125
Ulmus Glabra   125
Ulmus glabra tricuspida   125
Ulmus hollandica "Belgica"   125
Ulmus procera   125
Ulmus thomasii   125
United States of America   72
USS Constitution   47

V

Vendome   16,17,151,152
Venetian gothic   110
Victorian era   10,36,150
Virginia   xv,53,69,154,168,171,178, 185,187,190,192,196,206,216

W

Waban   98
Walden Pond   97
Wampanoag   24,26,49
warblers   2,32
Washington Street   30,37,77,78, 80,81,82

water lilies *35,105*
Water Street 90
Watertown 5,77
weeping European beech 124
weeping willow 20,125,126
West End 44
West Indies 50
westward migration 52
West Newton Street 114
Weymouth 26
wigwam 25
William Blaxton 26,29,48,163
William Howe 65,177,178,180
Wilmington and Brunswick 53

window to nowhere 8,9,10
winter 4,21,25,32,60,78,96,103, 116,122,126,127,128,129,134, 135,136,140,141,142,146
Winter Street 45,46,76,77,78,89, 106
women's rights activists 74
Worcester 58,88,89,189
wrens 2

Y

yellow throats 32
Yorktown xv,176,178

www.ingramcontent.com/pod-product-compliance
Lightning Source LLC
Chambersburg PA
CBHW070731160426
43192CB00009B/1402